COMPLETE GUIDE TO

Turning Pens & Pencils

Techniques and Projects for Turners of All Levels

COMPLETE GUIDE TO
Turning Pens & Pencils

Techniques and Projects for Turners of All Levels

Walter Hall

The Taunton Press

The Taunton Press
Inspiration for hands-on living®

The Taunton Press, Inc., 63 South Main Street, PO Box 5506, Newtown, CT 06470-5506
email: tp@taunton.com

First published 2011 by
Guild of Master Craftsman Publications Ltd
Castle Place, 166 High Street, Lewes,
East Sussex BN7 1XU

Publisher Jonathan Bailey
Production Manager Jim Bulley
Managing Editor Gerrie Purcell
Senior Project Editor Virginia Brehaut
Copy Editor Ian Whitelaw
Managing Art Editor Gilda Pacitti
Design Rob Janes/Fineline Studios
Pen Photography Andrew Perris

Library of Congress Cataloging-in-Publication Data

Hall, Walter, 1952-
  Complete guide to turning pens & pencils : techniques and projects for turners of all levels / author, Walter Hall.
    p. cm.
  ISBN 978-1-60085-365-4
  1. Turning (Lathe work) 2. Pens. I. Title.
  TT201.H2185 2011
  684'.083--dc23
                              2011020189

All other photography by the author except for the following: page 10 (top) and 12, Axminster; page 14 (top), Vicmarc; page 14 (bottom), Nick Arnull; page 20 (top left), Record Power; page 23 (top), Paul Dean; page 24 (top left), Anthony Bailey.

About Your Safety: Working wood is inherently dangerous. Using hand or power tools improperly or ignoring safety practices can lead to permanent injury or even death. Don't try to perform operations you learn about here (or elsewhere) unless you're certain they are safe for you. If something about an operation doesn't feel right, don't do it. Enjoy the craft, but keep safety foremost in your mind whenever you're in the shop.

Set in Myriad Pro
Color origination by GMC Reprographics
Printed and bound by Hung Hing Offset in China

CONTENTS

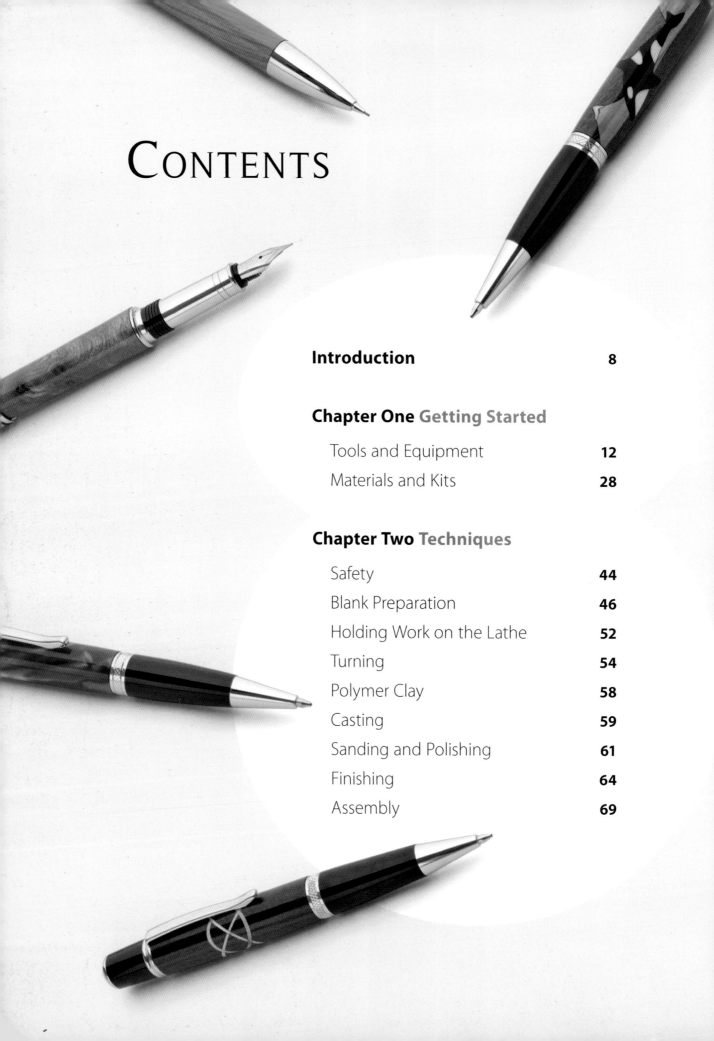

INTRODUCTION

Pen making using a wood-turning lathe is an absorbing pastime that can be as cheap and cheerful or as time consuming and expensive as you wish to make it. It is perfectly feasible to begin with only the purchase of a starter lathe and a few basic tools costing in total less than a couple of meals out in a decent restaurant, but on the other hand it is possible to spend thousands of dollars on fancy equipment and materials. In this book I have tried to explain what is required at the most basic level and also to give some indication of the astonishing range of tools, materials, and kits available in order to give newcomers to the hobby and those who are developing their skills the resources to make an informed choice.

As it is with cost so it is with skills. It is possible to make pens and pencils with only the most basic turning skills or to adopt more advanced techniques to suit your ability. If you can drill a straight hole in a pen blank and turn a cylinder to match the diameter of the bushings then you can make a pen, but as a more experienced maker you may wish to experiment with a range of techniques such as laminating, inlaying, clear casting, texturing, and perhaps even casting your own polyester resin blanks or adding patterns with an ornamental lathe such as the Beall Pen Wizard.

Over the 20 or more years that I have been making pens I have learned what will work for me and what will not. I have made countless mistakes and ruined lots of materials, and my intention when I started this book was to write a short guide to help beginners to the hobby to avoid some of the pitfalls and to benefit from my learning curve. It soon became clear that I had enough material to widen that ambition to cover a range of techniques and projects that I hope will enable most pen makers, whatever their skill level, to gain some benefit from my experience.

I have learned over the years that, as with so many things in life, there is no absolute right or wrong way to do most things related to pen making. As well as covering my own preferred methods of working, I have therefore tried to cover the alternatives that have been less successful for me but that other people find effective. I would, however, urge anyone new to the hobby to seek some instruction in basic turning skills either from a professional teacher or an experienced turner. Even a small lathe is a powerful machine tool and capable of causing serious injury if used incorrectly. Knowing how to use your tools properly will not only make your experience of pen making more enjoyable—it will also help to ensure that you enjoy it in safety.

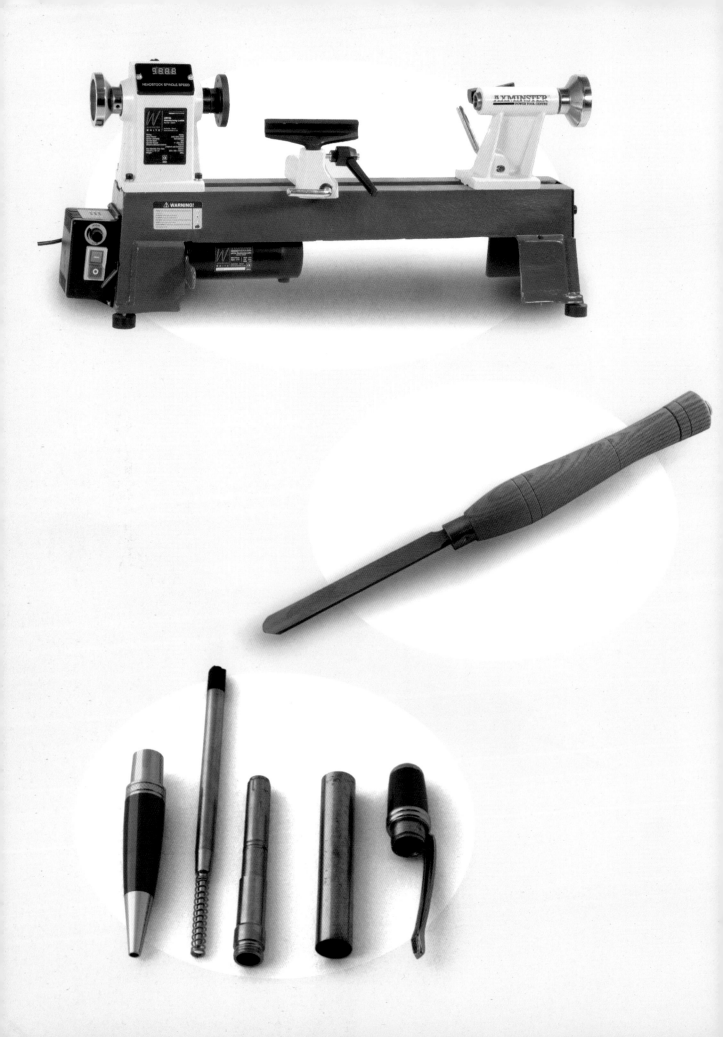

CHAPTER ONE
GETTING STARTED

TOOLS AND EQUIPMENT

Only a small range of tools is required to begin pen making. As you progress you may wish to acquire more specialized equipment and a wider range of accessories. In each of the following sections I have set out what is required and, where necessary, the alternative options available.

Lathes

Wood-turning lathes are available in all shapes and sizes, from the smallest, designed specifically for pen turning and other small work, to very large bowl turning lathes. Unless a lathe has been specifically designed for bowl turning and therefore does not have a bed or tailstock it can almost certainly be used for pen turning.

The lathe that you choose will depend upon what sort of turning you intend to undertake. If you plan to make only pens and other small items then a mini-lathe will serve your purpose, but if, like most turners, you plan to make a wide range of items including larger bowls and platters then a full-size lathe will be necessary.

If you already own a lathe you are happy with then please feel free to skip this section, but should you decide to upgrade your lathe or to buy a second lathe purely for pen turning then you will need to take the following factors into account.

Size

The size of lathe that you buy will depend not only upon the sort of work you intend to do, but also on the space you have available. When considering the space required for your lathe, remember to take into account any extra room required for swiveling heads or outboard attachments. Few things are more tiresome than having to move the whole lathe every time you want to swivel the headstock to turn outboard. A small benchtop lathe for pen making, such as the one shown here **A**, need not take up a great deal of space and is small enough to be stored away when not in use.

Power

The power of a lathe motor is usually measured in horsepower (hp) but sometimes in watts. Conversion between the two forms of measurement in order to compare lathes can be complex but for the purposes of selecting a lathe it is reasonable to estimate that 750 watts is approximately equal

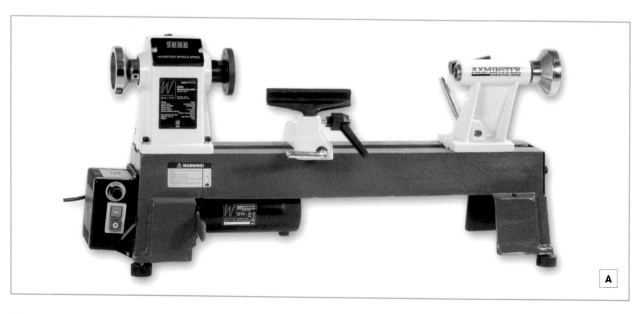

A

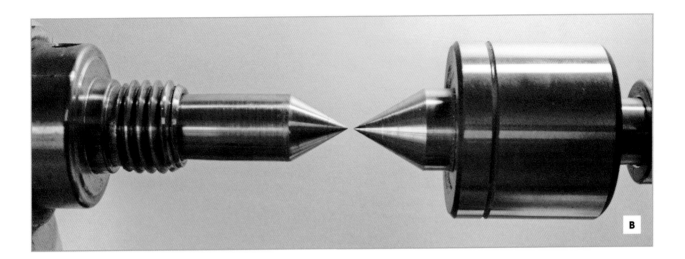

to 1 hp. A lathe for turning only pens does not need to be very powerful and a mini-lathe with a ¼ hp motor will be more than adequate, but for bowl turning and other work, the more powerful the lathe the better, with a 1hp motor being the minimum that I would consider adequate for a medium-size lathe.

Speed

The speeds required for wood turning are dependent upon the diameter of the piece being turned. There are many formulas for calculating the appropriate speed but a simple rule of thumb is to divide 6,000 by the diameter in inches of what you are turning, which gives you the required speed in revolutions per minute (rpm). (The metric equivalent of this calculation is to divide 15,250 by the diameter in centimeters.) Thus a 12-in. (300mm)-diameter bowl should be turned at 500 rpm while a 1-in. (25-mm)-diameter pen blank could be turned at up to 6,000 rpm. Most lathes have a maximum speed of 2,000-3,000 rpm, so pens can usually be turned at full speed. The most important consideration, if you plan larger work, is to ensure the lathe has a low enough minimum speed.

Variable speed or belt changing

Lathe speed is changed either by moving the position of the drive belt on the motor and spindle pulleys or by means of a mechanical or electronic variable speed mechanism. Some lathes have an electronically variable speed mechanism as well as movable belt positions, giving several speed ranges. Changing the belt position can be fiddly and time consuming, and while this is more important for larger work, a lathe with a variable speed mechanism can save a great deal of time even for the pen turner. Electronic variable speed systems are often more reliable than the mechanical systems, which usually depend upon expanding pulleys.

Threads and tapers

While lathe spindles come in a wide range of different thread sizes, most chucking systems have interchangeable inserts or backing plates that can be changed to suit the thread of your lathe spindle, so apart from avoiding obscure sizes that are difficult to find matching components for, the thread size need not unduly influence your choice. Most lathes, other than huge industrial ones, will also have a No. 1 or No. 2 Morse taper in the head and tailstocks. It is of little significance which you choose, just as long as you match your mandrels and centers to the taper of your lathe. Of course, if you are replacing an existing lathe you may want to choose one with a Morse taper and spindle thread that matches your present lathe in order to avoid the cost of replacing ancillary equipment.

Quality

The quality of modern lathes is generally very good. Even relatively inexpensive machines imported from the Far East will provide adequate performance for the amateur turner. If you are serious about your pen making, however, you will want the best quality lathe you can afford within your budget. One of the most important factors in making quality pens is the concentricity of the pen barrels, which is dependent upon ensuring that the lathe, the mandrels, and other fittings that you are using are running true. The quality of the lathe bearings and the accuracy of the alignment of the head and tailstocks are crucial to ensuring true running. The latter can be checked by putting centers into the head and tailstocks and bringing them together to see that they align exactly and run true to one another when the lathe is turned on **B**.

Of course, your budget will be a major factor in making a decision, but for the pen maker it would make much more sense to purchase a small but high-quality mini-lathe **C** than to spend the same amount of money on a larger but less well-engineered product.

C

Features of a typical lathe

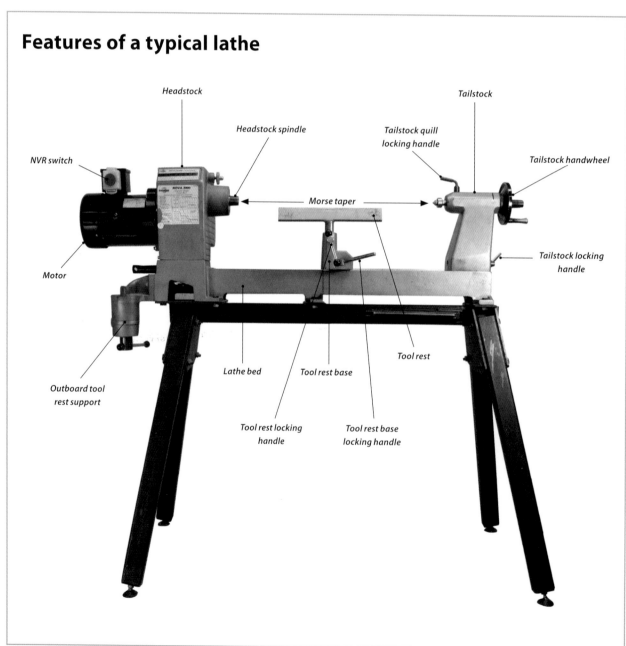

Headstock

Headstock spindle

Tailstock

Tailstock quill locking handle

NVR switch

Tailstock handwheel

Morse taper

Motor

Tailstock locking handle

Outboard tool rest support

Tool rest

Lathe bed

Tool rest base

Tool rest locking handle

Tool rest base locking handle

Mandrels and holding work

The mandrel **A** is the most common means by which the pen blank is held on the lathe. It consists of an accurately machined steel rod that is mounted by means of a chuck or Morse taper fitting in the headstock of the lathe. Mandrels come in two sizes, known as A and B mandrels or 7mm and 8mm mandrels. The metric dimensions refer not to the diameter of the mandrel shaft itself but to the outside diameter of the standard brass pen tube that will fit the mandrel.

Pens with tubes of a larger diameter than 8mm are mounted using bushings that are bored to fit the mandrel and machined to fit the inside diameter of the pen tube. By far the majority of modern pen kits use bushings that are designed to fit the A-type mandrel.

The end of the mandrel is threaded to take a knob or nut that is tightened to hold the blanks and bushings in place and is machined with a dimple in the end of the shaft to engage with a revolving center in the lathe tailstock.

Some makers prefer to mount the pen blank by holding the bushings directly between centers, with a 60° dead center in the headstock and a 60° live center in the tailstock. Some specialized kits also require dedicated fittings specifically designed for the purpose; these methods are explained where necessary in the project sections. In this section, I explain the various types of standard mandrel mounting and the advantages and disadvantages of each.

A fixed mandrel has the shaft permanently attached to a Morse taper. It is designed to mount both barrels of a two-part pen kit simultaneously and if a kit with a single barrel is mounted then an additional bushing is required to pack out the mandrel. The main advantage of these mandrels is their cheapness and simplicity, and if they are used with care there is little to go wrong with them. However, the lack of any adjustment when mounting single barrels means that they are more prone to whip and vibration and are therefore potentially less accurate than other forms of mandrel.

A

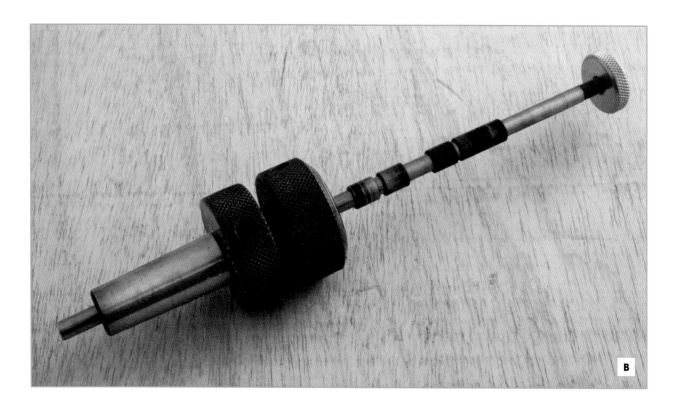

The length of the mandrel will also tend to magnify the impact of any inaccuracy in the alignment of the lathe head and tailstocks, resulting in an oval-shaped barrel.

An adjustable mandrel **B** has a shaft mounted in a Morse taper fitting that, by means of a grub screw or collet-type mechanism, can be loosened so that the shaft can be slid in and out and adjusted to suit the length of the blank that is being worked on. These mandrels are less prone to inaccuracy than the fixed mandrels, but the shorter length may mean that a shorter tool rest must be fitted to the lathe.

A drill driver is a split Morse taper fitting designed to grip a mandrel shaft as the tailstock is tightened against the end of the shaft. Drill drivers share the advantages and disadvantages of fixed mandrels but have the additional advantage that several mandrel shafts can be used interchangeably.

A collet chuck **C** is by far the most accurate means of holding a mandrel shaft in the headstock; it retains the shaft in standard interchangeable collets and may be either a Morse taper fitting or a screw fitting to match the thread of the lathe spindle. As with an adjustable mandrel, the length of the shaft can be set to suit the workpiece.

A Jacobs-type chuck or keyless Morse taper chuck can also be used to hold a standard mandrel shaft accurately, but these lack the adjustment facility of the collet chuck.

A split mandrel consists of two parts that fit into the ends of the pen barrel. One is held in a drill driver fitting or a chuck and the other is retained by the revolving center in the tailstock. These can make mounting and removing the barrels a little quicker but are seldom used now that adjustable and collet chuck mandrels are readily available.

C

Finally in this section, I will mention a recently introduced device known as a mandrel saver **D**. This is a revolving center drilled to fit a standard mandrel and it is used instead of the mandrel nut to retain the components on the mandrel. The action of bringing up the tailstock quill tightens the bushings and blanks onto the shaft. This can help to reduce inaccuracies caused by the shaft bending under pressure from the tailstock.

D

Technical **tip**

If you take good care of your mandrels they will last for many years. They require little maintenance; only occasional cleaning of the shaft and Morse taper, and a light brushing to keep the working parts free from accumulated sawdust or adhesive residues. Spraying with camellia oil will help to prevent rust without marking wooden blanks.

Drill bits

Drill bits come in a wide variety of types and each is designed for a particular purpose. Only a few are suitable for drilling pen blanks and the type of bit selected will depend upon the material to be drilled.

Standard twist drill bits are not primarily designed for drilling wood but will nonetheless work reasonably effectively in straight-grained hardwoods and are perfectly adequate for synthetic materials such as acrylic and Corian®. If you are making only a few pens and already have a set of twist drills then you will get by with care, but if you plan to take your pen making seriously then you should consider some of the alternatives.

Brad point bits **A**, often simply described as wood bits, have, as their name suggests, a long sharp point that helps to maintain the course of the drill through the grain of the wood, as well as shaped wings to cut an accurate hole. This makes them an excellent choice for timber blanks, especially those with a wild grain.

Bullet point bits **B** are my personal choice for drilling all pen-making materials. They are a cross between a twist bit and a brad point bit, having a more robust bullet-shaped point that helps prevent the bit from wandering. They work equally effectively in wood, metal, synthetics, and natural materials such as horn and antler.

Dedicated pen drill bits are now available in many of the sizes required for common pen kits. These bits have a complex shape ground into the tip, which is designed to ensure accuracy, and they are usually 150mm long to enable drilling of longer blanks. If you make many pens you may find these an invaluable asset, though they run a little expensive for the occasional user.

For some specialized kits with shaped components it may be advisable to purchase special stepped drill bits designed to drill a hole to an exact fit, although the occasional maker may get by with normal drill bits and a considerable amount of care.

Drilling equipment

It is not possible to drill pen blanks accurately with a handheld drill. No matter how steady your hand, you will likely end up with a hole that is not centred in the blank or a hole that is oval rather than round. The drill bit and the blank need to be held steady and in true alignment with one another. This can be achieved on the lathe, in a drill press, or with a power drill mounted in a vertical stand.

My favorite method is to drill the blanks on the lathe **C**; I find this provides the most consistent accuracy. For drilling in the lathe you will need a chuck with suitable jaws to hold the blank in the headstock. Suitable chuck jaws would include pin jaws and engineering jaws designed to work in compression mode. Dedicated pen blank drilling chucks are also available with jaws designed for the purpose.

You will also require a Jacobs chuck, collet chuck, or other drill chuck to hold the drill bit in the tailstock. The type of chuck used is less important than its accuracy, so it pays to buy the best chucks you can afford.

A drill press is another good way of drilling accurate blanks. If you are purchasing a drill press, pay particular attention to the length of travel. Most small drill presses are designed for precision engineering work and may not have enough capacity to drill right through a pen blank in one pass.

C

If you already have a drill press then you may already have a dedicated vise or cross vise to hold the blank. If not then you will need to either make or purchase a suitable vise or clamp to keep the blank vertical. A simple clamp can be made by joining two wooden jaws with a V-shape cut into each. Alternatively, special pen blank vises are available commercially, but in my opinion these are no more effective than a shopmade clamp.

Of course, you do not need an expensive drill press just to drill pen blanks. A vertical stand for your power drill will do the job just fine, but do make sure you purchase a good solid stand and use it with a vise or clamp just as you would with a drill press. I used this power drill and stand **D** fitted with a cheap cross vise for many years and found it most effective. Pen making can be as cheap or expensive as you choose to make it.

D

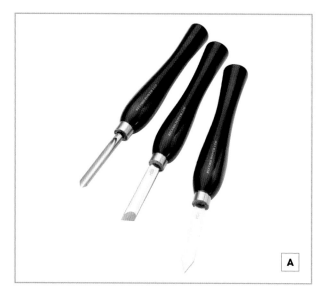

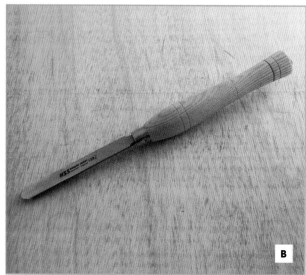

Chisels and gouges

Unlike many other branches of woodturning, pen making does not require a large number of cutting tools or the maintenance of specially shaped grinds. I can produce a simple slimline pen with straight barrels from a square blank using only a 1-in. (25-mm) spindle roughing gouge or a ¾-in. (20-mm) skew chisel, and there is no reason why anyone should not be able to do the same with a little practice.

Apart from a spindle roughing gouge or similar shallow fluted gouge and a skew chisel, the only other cutting tools that are essential are a ⅛-in. (3-mm) or ³⁄₁₆-in. (5-mm) parting tool and a small (about ⅜-in. [10-mm]) spindle gouge.

The final choice of tools comes down to individual preference. Some makers prefer to use smaller tools such as a ½-in. (13-mm) shallow gouge and a ½-in. (13-mm) skew chisel, and it is possible to buy sets of these smaller tools specifically designed for pen turning . I am more comfortable working with larger tools. The table shows my choice of essentials, together with alternatives for those who prefer working with smaller tools. I also occasionally use a ½-in. (13-mm) round skew chisel with a shallow skew angle.

Most quality tools manufactured today are made from M2 high-speed steel (hss) or variants of this material designed to enhance the edge-holding properties of the tool. Older or cheaper tools may be made from carbon steel, which can be sharpened to a finer/sharper cutting edge but does not hold an edge as long as the M2 hss tools. My advice would be to buy the best quality tools you can afford from one of the well-known and respected brands. Fine work is more easily achieved with fine tools.

Tool sizes for pen making

	My choice	Smaller alternative
Shallow gouge (for roughing blanks)	1-in. (25-mm) or ¾-in. (20-mm)	½-in. (13-mm)
Skew chisel (for finishing cuts)	¾-in. (20-mm) oval skew chisel	½-in. (13-mm) ova oblong skew chisel
Parting tool (for cutting steps or grooves in blanks to fit rings or bands)	³⁄₁₆-in. (5-mm) diamond parting tool	⅛-in. (3-mm) or ⁵⁄₃₂-in. (4-mm) parting tool
Deep fluted gouge (for beading or coving and cutting small details)	⅜-in. (10-mm)	⅜-in. (10-mm) or ¼-in. (6-mm)

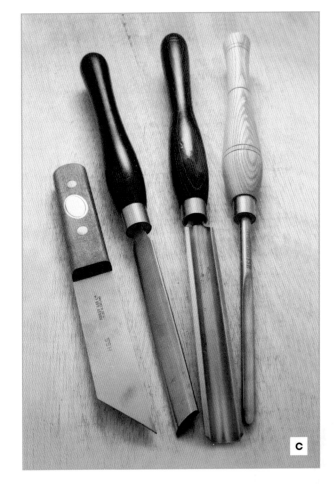

One further tool that I will mention is the Spindlemaster **B** , which is designed primarily for those who find using a skew chisel difficult. It is, however, an extremely useful tool for turning acrylic materials.

Sharpening tools

No matter how good the quality of your tools, they will be useless unless they are kept sharp and in good condition **C** . The sharpening of tools is a special skill in its own right and the focus of much debate among woodworkers of all disciplines. Whole books have been written on the subject and it is not my intention here to describe all the possible means of achieving a razor-sharp and long-lasting edge. I shall set out the principles of what we are seeking to achieve and describe what works for me, but if you are already a woodworker you may have your own methods. If not, over time you will find and adopt the methods that suit you best.

In sharpening wood-turning tools what we are seeking to do is maintain the shape of the tool while producing an edge that is as sharp as possible. A sharp edge is achieved where the two planes of the tool (back or flute and ground edge) meet. The smoother and more polished the surfaces, the finer the edge. The finer the edge, the sharper the tool. Polishing the back or flute will help to achieve a sharp edge as it will improve the quality of the surface where the two planes meet.

New tools are supplied with the bevel preground, and for pen-making work there is no need to diverge from the manufacturer's standard grind. If you buy old tools you may need to regrind the bevel to a suitable angle. For gouges this should be between 40° and 30° and for skew chisels about 40°. The angle of the skew can be anywhere between 15° and 30°.

While it is possible to grind a gouge by hand, this is an acquired skill and beginners would be best advised to either seek instruction from an experienced turner or purchase one of the many jigs available for use with a bench grinder.

I only use a bench grinder when tools need reshaping or have been damaged. Routine sharpening is done using a vertical wet grinder and final honing by hand with diamond hones. I hone my tools regularly in use and resharpen only after several hours use. My ½-in. (13-mm) round skew chisel has never been near a grinding machine of any sort since it was manufactured. I maintain the edge with medium and fine diamond hones.

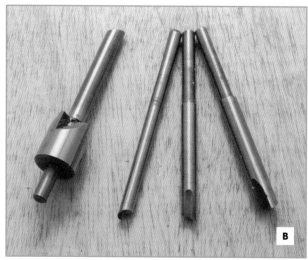

Blank (or barrel) trimmers

One of the most important requirements in making a good-quality pen is to create a good fit between the turned pen barrels and the metal components. This can only be achieved if the end of the blank is trimmed neatly and exactly square to the tube.

Blanks can be trimmed using a disk sander, but great care is required in achieving squareness, especially if the bore in which the brass tube is fitted is not parallel with the sides of the blank. This can be overcome with the use of a purpose-designed jig **A** that works with the sander's miter fence. With some brittle materials a disk sander may be the preferred method to avoid chipping or breaking away, but for the most part I prefer to use a blank trimmer.

A blank trimmer consists of a shaft on which is mounted a cylindrical cutting head. The shaft is inserted into the brass tube and the cutter turned against the end of the blank thus ensuring a perfectly square end. In order to ensure absolute squareness it is important that the shaft is a good fit in the tube and the better trimmers **B** have interchangeable shafts and sleeves to suit different sizes of barrel. For those that do not it is easy to make a turned wooden or acrylic sleeve, bored to fit the shaft of the trimmer and turned to fit exactly inside the brass tube.

A blank trimmer can be mounted in a chuck in a slowly turning lathe and the blank held in a clamp, or alternatively you can hold the blank in a vise and use the trimmer mounted in a cordless drill. Other options, if only light trimming is required, are to mount the chuck in the tailstock and turn the blank against the trimmer by hand or to make a handle for the trimmer with an old chuck **C** and complete the operation entirely by hand.

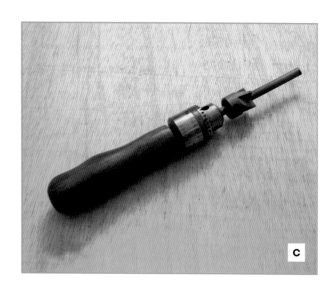

Assembly tools

The final stage of pen production is the assembly of the components, which are a press fit into the tubes. Hours of painstaking work can be destroyed at this stage by careless fitting, which can cause the barrels to crack or split. To achieve a perfect assembly it is essential to ensure not only that the tubes are free from glue and other contaminants that may cause an obstruction, but also that each component is square to the brass tube and that it is pressed smoothly and firmly into the barrel.

This can be achieved with care using a bench vise or, alternatively, you can use one of the many commercially available pen presses **A** designed especially for the job.

My preferred method is to use the lathe as a pen press. I have made wooden inserts for the Morse tapers of my lathe **B** and by placing the components between the head and tailstock I can press them into place by gently bringing up the tailstock quill. These inserts are easy to make, but you can also buy ready-made ones that are manufactured from a resilient but nondamaging synthetic material.

Technical **tip**

Firm, but carefully applied, pressure is the key to good assembly. After making sure that the brass tubes are free from glue residues or other obstructions, carefully align the components and press the parts into place using your chosen assembly tool. Steady pressure will ensure that they remain aligned and avoid placing stresses on the sides of the tubes that can cause splitting.

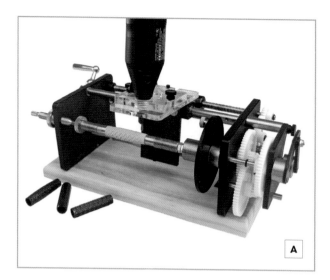

A

B

The Beall Pen Wizard

The Pen Wizard **A** is an ornamental pen lathe that can be used to add designs to the turned barrels of pens in the form of spirals, wave patterns, or flats. A multi-tool, or a suspended motor, with a flexible shaft fitted with suitable burrs or router bits is needed to make the cuts. The pen blanks to be worked upon are held in place on a standard threaded mandrel supplied with the machine; this is mounted on an index plate that is used to determine the number and placement of the cuts.

The index plate is driven by a gearbox with interchangeable gears **B**, which in turn is driven by the lead screw to which the cutting tool mounting plate is fitted. By turning the handle of the lead screw, the cutting tool and blank are moved in relation to one another according to the gearbox settings. By varying the gearbox settings, the speed at which the blank revolves in relation to the transit of the cutter can be altered, thereby determining the shape of the spiral created. The number and spacing of the spirals is determined by moving the mandrel and blank in relation to the 24 holes in the index plate.

In addition, there is a reversing mechanism that enables the user to cut spirals both clockwise and anti-clockwise, and a "guilloche" mechanism that causes the gearbox to move the index plate in a side to side movement rather than in a continuous circle, thereby creating wave patterns instead of spirals. This device is adjustable so that the amplitude and frequency of the waves can be varied.

If all of this sounds complicated, this is because the Pen Wizard is a complex machine and the functioning is rather more difficult to explain in words than it is to demonstrate. The machine is supplied with a comprehensive manual and DVD that enable the new user quickly to become acquainted with the possibilities. There is also a demonstration video available online at the manufacturer's Web site (www.bealltool.com).

The photos on the facing page show some examples of the possibilities for creating decorative pens using this machine. The Pen Wizard is an expensive and specialized tool but for the enthusiastic pen maker who wishes to explore alternative pen designs it is a unique and invaluable asset.

A desk pen textured with a multi-tool and given a spiral pattern of hollows using a core box router bit in the Pen Wizard **C**.

A pen with the grip patterned with spiral grooves **D**.

A Slimline pencil with spiral patterned barrels **E**.

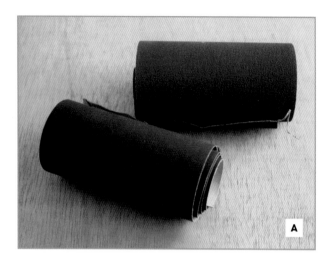

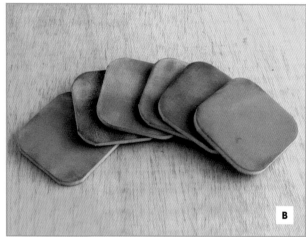

Abrasives

Modern abrasives come in what can seem a bewildering range of types, and it is important to use the appropriate abrasive for the material you are working with in order to achieve the best results.

Although abrasives come in other forms, such as bonded grinding wheels or metal cutting disks, these are not of concern to us for finishing pens. The abrasives I describe here are coated abrasives, which are bonded to a flexible backing of paper or cloth, micromesh cushioned abrasive sheets and pads, and nonwoven nylon abrasives, which are of most use to the pen turner in the form of pads.

Coated abrasives are differentiated by five factors—the abrasive material, the backing type and weight, the bonding adhesive, and the coating. All types of abrasive are available in a range of grit sizes—the higher the number, the finer the grit. Of the many abrasive materials available, perhaps the most useful as a general-purpose sanding medium for both wood and acrylic is aluminum oxide. Silicone carbide, found in the wet-or-dry sandpaper used in car body repairs, can be useful for acrylics but is prone to stain light-colored woods with dark abrasive particles.

The backing is not terribly significant in terms of performance for our purposes, so this is largely a matter of personal choice. Paper-backed abrasives are cheaper but more prone to tearing in use, while the more expensive flexible cloth backings are more robust and may last longer. My personal choice for a general abrasive A is a lightweight, flexible, cloth-backed aluminum oxide material available from woodworking retailers. Like most aluminum oxide abrasives this is available in the following range of grits: 80, 120, 150, 180, 240, 320, and 400. A cheaper but effective choice would be medium-weight paper-backed aluminum oxide abrasive.

Micromesh abrasives are made from abrasive crystals that float on the backing material. They have no coating and the bond that holds the crystals to the backing is flexible. They also have very even abrasive particles and this, combined with their flexibility, results in a very fine scratch pattern. They are available in grits ranging from 1,500 to 12,000, and the finest grades will produce a polished finish on acrylics or on a hard material such as cyanoacrylate (CA) or lacquer. Available as cushioned pads B or flexible sheets, micromesh abrasives can be used wet or dry. Used wet they quickly bring acrylics to a fine polish.

Nonwoven nylon abrasives are open-weave nylon materials coated with abrasive. They, too, are useful for fine finishing and have the advantage that they can be washed out and reused.

Finishes

Pens and pencils that are made from natural timber or laser-cut blanks require a protective finish **A** . Polymer clays require some form of protection, either with a hard finish or a wax. Synthetic materials, animal horn, and some laminated and stabilized blanks can be brought to a fine finish by polishing and require nothing more that an occasional coat of microcrystalline wax to keep them looking pristine.

One of the simplest finishes to apply is friction polish, which is a form of French polish that dries by the heat caused by friction during application to the revolving work. It can be applied to bare wood or over shellac or cellulose-based sanding sealer. It can also be applied over a melamine or cellulose lacquer. Wax finishes can be applied over friction polish to give added protection. Its main advantage is its ease of application but it is not as robust as some other finishes and will show signs of wear after much handling.

Melamine or cellulose lacquers are harder wearing than friction polishes but require more care in application on the lathe as they dry very quickly. When applied in this way they require polishing with micromesh or on a buffing wheel to achieve a good finish. They can also be applied by spraying after the work is removed from the lathe but, again, care is needed. If applied too thickly, they will run or sag, and thick coatings of these materials can look plasticky.

Close-grained timbers can be polished with compounds such as Tripoli and white diamond on buffing wheels **B** and then protected with a wax finish. This works well with textured pieces or work that has been patterned using the Beall Pen Wizard and other finishes can be difficult to apply. A disadvantage is the need to maintain the wax finish.

Cut and polish pastes containing Tripoli or similar abrasives are also available for use on work while still on the lathe, after sanding with fine-grit abrasives. As with buffing compounds, these require a wax finish to be applied for protection and are dependent upon the wax finish to maintain the appearance of the pen.

Oil finishes are popular with wood turners for larger items such as bowls and vases and in these applications they can be very effective. I do not, however, recommend oil finishes for pens and pencils as they do not stand up well to the heavy handling that writing instruments receive, although a wipe with boiled linseed oil will bring out the figure in the wood before applying another finish.

One of the most frequently used finishes for pens is cyanoacrylate (CA). While the primary function of CA is as an adhesive (instant glue), being a form of acrylic it makes an extremely effective and hardwearing finish. It can be applied on its own or with boiled linseed oil. I prefer to apply it without the oil, but I apply a coat of cellulose sanding sealer or a wipe of boiled linseed oil first. Despite my initial reservations about using an adhesive as a finish, I have yet to find anything that provides such a high gloss or is equally hardwearing. Application is not difficult with a little practice. As with lacquers, polishing with micromesh and buffing are required to achieve a high gloss.

As a final protective coat I give a finishing polish to all my pens with a thin coat of microcrystalline wax buffed with a soft cloth. This not only protects the shine but also helps to prevent fingerprints from spoiling the appearance of the finished pen.

MATERIALS AND KITS

When I started out making pens, the range of materials and kits available was limited. Nowadays it is possible to buy a huge variety of kits, from the most basic ballpoint to high-end fountain pens, and the selection of materials and ready-prepared barrel blanks means you need never make two pens the same. The following sections describe some of the options available.

Wood

Of all the materials available for pen making, my favorite is wood in all its varieties. My interest in working with wood and my love of the material were what originally got me into turning and led to my passion for pen making. Of course, as it is a natural material, working with wood can be frustrating. Many hours of work can be destroyed by an unnoticed split or fault in a wooden blank that does not manifest itself until the pen or pencil is nearing completion, but the satisfaction gained from completing a pen in a highly figured wood or burl **A** more than compensates for any such annoyances.

There are, I believe, more than 40,000 wood species, and while not all are suitable for pen making, the choice is sufficient to ensure that one need never run out of ideas. What is more, every piece of wood is unique, so no two pens you make in this material will ever be identical.

In choosing wood for pen making there are a number of factors to consider. The first of these is the suitability of the stock. Wood for making pen blanks must be properly dried and stable. Green wood will move, shrink, and crack as it dries. Take care, too, when selecting prepared blanks to check for cracks and defects, and when cutting your own blanks from larger pieces of wood try to cut away any defective parts. It is often necessary to strike a balance between attractive figure in a piece and ensuring its integrity when drilling and turning. Sometimes highly figured wood and burls may even need to be stabilized in order to ensure they remain intact. This can be done with resin-type wood hardeners, cyanoacrylate (CA) glue, or lacquer, or by using more advanced techniques that are beyond the scope of this book but are easily researched by typing "stabilizing wood" into an Internet search engine.

A

B

Here we have a mixed selection of native and exotic woods, including English sycamore and yew, Spanish olivewood, teak and ziricote from South America, and pohutukawa from New Zealand.

Next you may wish to consider the ease with which the wood can be worked. Some of the harder and more brittle species can be disheartening for a beginner. When I first started out it was frustrating when I could not even manage to drill a 7-mm hole through a snakewood blank without it splitting. Of course, poor technique was the cause and much work with more forgiving woods was required before I learned to use slow speeds and withdraw the bit regularly to clear the flutes. However, the beginner may still wish to choose more easily worked wood, such as fruitwoods like apple and cherry, before graduating to more difficult species.

Finally you will need to consider the appearance of the pen or pencil you wish to make. Will the kit look best with a dark- or light-colored wood? Does the style of the pen require a highly figured stock or would a plainer species make it less fussy? What will best suit the plating you have chosen? For whom is the pen intended and what will suit their taste? Is the pen to be decorated with texturing or spiral work **B** ? If so, a less highly figured stock may work best.

Stabilized wood and laminated materials

Some wood species, particularly burls, are fragile and can be difficult to work with, so in order to make them more usable they are sometimes stabilized by impregnating them with other materials. Pen-turning blanks that have been treated with resins, acrylics, and other chemicals under pressure are available and these can provide attractive and unusual alternatives to natural timber. Often dyes are used to enhance or color these blanks, too.

Stabilized blanks, because of the additives, have a tendency to take the edge off tools more rapidly than ordinary woods, so frequent honing is recommended. It is, however, easier to achieve a good finish from the tool with these materials than with an untreated burl, and they can often be finished in the same way as acrylics just by polishing with micromesh and buffing with polishing compounds without the need for any further finish.

Another interesting alternative to natural timber is laminated material **A** . Rather like plywood, but with different colored layers, this material is available under a number of different trade names, such as DymondWood®, Tigerwood, and ColorWood®, but all share a similar laminated structure made up from layers of dyed veneers and cross or diagonally cut in various ways to present different patterns when included in a finished pen or pencil.

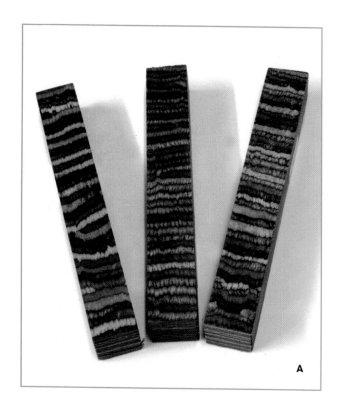

A

Like stabilized wood, laminated blanks contain adhesives and other substances that will cause tools to dull more readily, but they, too, can be finished by polishing with micromesh and buffing with polishing compounds, and in many cases they respond well to wet sanding.

Technical **tip**

I usually wear a face mask or respirator to protect against the dust that is created when sanding pen-making materials, but stabilized wood and laminated materials contain high levels of adhesives and other chemicals so I always pay particular attention to ensuring that I am protected from the dust created when working with them. Using a dust extractor along with any respiratory protection is good practice. Remember to protect yourself when cleaning up the workshop afterwards too.

Synthetics

In this section I use the generic term synthetics to describe a wide range of man-made materials that are available in the form of pen blanks or in forms that can be converted into pen blanks. They include alternatives to natural materials such as ivory and tortoiseshell (which are no longer legally available), cast acrylic and polyester materials in a wide range of colors and styles, clear casting resins, and the solid surface materials such as Corian that are used for kitchen countertops.

Alternatives to natural materials are manufactured from cast polyester and have working properties similar to, but a little more forgiving than, most of the other acrylic materials, being a little softer and less brittle than acrylics. They are available in a wide range of designs to replicate antler, horn, ivory, bone, tortoiseshell, and many others. As well as being kinder to the environment than the materials they replace, these materials are often more consistent and pleasant to work with. Cast polyester blanks are also available in many of the styles described below for acrylics.

Cast acrylics

Cast acrylic materials come in a vast range of styles and colors **A** that includes brightly colored abstract designs, replicas of semiprecious materials such as coral, jade, and onyx, animal print designs, and crushed velvet. These materials can be worked with the same high-speed steel tools that we use for turning wooden blanks and drilled using ordinary twist drills or my preferred option of bullet point bits. When turning these materials, sharp tools and light cuts are essential to avoid either overheating or melting the material or chipping and breakout. Drilling should be done at low speeds and the bit should be withdrawn frequently to ensure accuracy and to avoid problems caused by overheating the blank.

Clear casting resins

These are epoxy-based resins that are mixed with a catalyst (hardener) to create crystal clear blanks in which various items can be embedded for decorative effect. Commercially available clear cast blanks include material such as snake skins,

computer circuit boards  **B** , feathers **C** , and even shredded dollar bills. These blanks come already cast around the tube for various types of pen kit. It is also quite possible to cast your own unique blanks using any materials you choose—the possibilities are limited only by your imagination. Project No. 14 (see p. 132) explains how to cast your own clear blanks.

Clear cast resins have similar working properties to acrylics and require the same level of care and tool sharpness to obtain good results.

Solid surface materials

Originally designed to create countertops in kitchens and laboratories etc., these come in a range of colors often intended to replicate natural stone. While they can be bought as prepared pen blanks, a much cheaper option is to obtain offcuts from a local kitchen installer. As with the other synthetic materials, they can be worked with normal wood turning tools. They finish well with micromesh abrasives and can be wet sanded.

Technical **tip**

All of the materials described in this section can be glued to the brass pen tubes using cyanoacrylate or epoxy adhesives and all can be finished by sanding, polishing, and buffing without the need for a separate finish.

Polymer clay

Despite its name, polymer clay is not a mineral-based material at all—it is a synthetic material based on polyvinyl chloride (PVC). Like natural clay, it can be sculpted, rolled, and molded into a wide range of shapes. Once it has been baked in an oven or kiln it hardens and can be drilled, machined, or worked with turning tools, and sanded and polished to a fine finish.

Although it has not been widely exploited as a pen-making medium, polymer clay provides an interesting range of options for the pen maker. It is available as ready-made and baked turning blanks premolded onto brass tubes, as premade "canes" of the millefiori type **A** , and as colored blocks or sheets of clay **B** . Those with the necessary skill can also make their own millefiori canes.

The pre-prepared blanks turn easily and are rather similar in their working properties to polyester blanks. Care must be taken, however, not to turn at too high a speed, as this can cause overheating and softening. They can be sanded and then polished with a buffing wheel and white diamond compound or finished with a cyanoacrylate finish if preferred.

The canes or sheets of clay can be worked and used to wrap the brass tubes and then baked. These blanks can be made to the finished size required for the kit to be used or they can be made oversize and turned down to fit. Project No. 8 (see page 104) describes both of these methods.

Technical **tip**

To add variety when working with polymer clay canes you can create smaller versions of the pattern by gently rolling one end of the cane to create a thinner section. Slicing through this reduced cross-section will give a smaller image that is otherwise identical to the original.

Laser-cut blanks

Modern laser-cutting technology has given rise to the laser-cut blank. These are made using a laser-cutting device fitted with a rotating shaft that enables extremely complex shapes to be cut into cylindrical blanks. The earliest blanks of this type were in the form of flags and jigsaw puzzles, but the range available now extends to include themes as diverse as golfing and polar bears. Each blank is made up from a number of separate components, cut from dyed and stabilized wood, that must be assembled and glued together by the user to form a pattern or picture **A**.

Laser-cut blanks allow the maker to create pens that would be extremely difficult to make by any other means **B**. However, this should not be taken to imply that they are an easy option, and for the maker who sells his pens and pencils, the cost of these blanks makes for an expensive finished product. They are, however, extremely enjoyable to assemble and turn, and the resulting pens and pencils are very attractive.

A degree of dexterity is required to make up a laser-cut kit into a finished blank—the components are a neat fit to each other and some can be very tiny. Holding some parts in place while others are located can be a challenge, and the opportunities for gluing your hands to the work or the work to the bench are extensive. I wear disposable latex gloves and use tweezers or fine-nosed pliers to handle the smaller components. Each laser-cut kit comes with comprehensive instructions for assembly, and as each is different it is important to follow these carefully. Project No. 12 (see page 122) shows how to make up, turn, and finish a Sierra-style pen using a laser-cut blank that depicts a killer whale.

Natural materials

Other materials that can be used for pen making include animal-based materials such as horn, antler and bone and some of the softer minerals such as soapstone. Some materials, such as ivory, are no longer considered environmentally acceptable, and man-made substitutes should be used.

Deer, moose, and other antler-bearing animals shed their antlers each year, so there is a ready supply of this material. Being a bony material, antler is harder than wood and also more abrasive, so while normal tools can be used, they must be sharp and will need regular honing as work progresses. Antler is also porous, so care is needed when drilling to avoid wandering of the bit, and the pores need to be filled by flooding with thin CA adhesive by capillary action. Once filled, the material may be brought to a high polish by sanding and buffing without the need for any applied finish.

Horn from animals such as water buffalo A is a keratin- and bone-based substance with characteristics similar to some plastic materials. Unlike antlers, which are shed annually, horns develop throughout the life of the animal. Like antler, horn can be turned with normal turning tools but it is not porous, so filling is not required. Horn can also be finished by sanding and polishing using micromesh and buffing compounds and does not require the application of a finish.

Some minerals are soft enough to be turned using the high-speed steel tools used for wood turning. Soapstone B for example is available in many attractive natural colors, drills, turns very well, and can be brought to a fine finish.

When obtaining natural materials for pen making, please be aware of, and take care to protect, the environment and the species with which we share the planet. Do make sure that your materials were obtained from a sustainable source and that no poaching, cruelty, or unnecessary killing was involved in their acquisition.

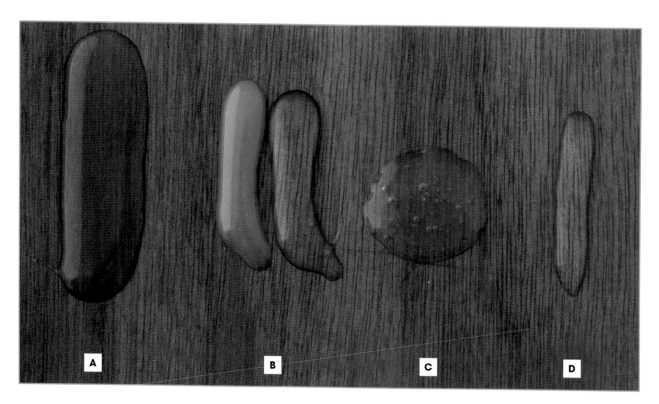

Adhesives

Adhesives are used in pen making primarily to glue the blanks to the brass tubes that form the structure of the pen or pencil. Cyanoacrylate (CA) and epoxy glues are also used in the assembly of laser-cut blank kits and cyanoacrylate adhesive can be used as a finish as described earlier (see page 27). Polyurethane (PU) adhesives can also be used for gluing the tubes.

For gluing blanks to the tubes, each type of adhesive has advantages and disadvantages. The choice of which to use for a particular project will depend upon a number of factors, including what is most suitable for the type of blank and your personal preference for ease of use, drying time etc.

Polyurethane

Polyurethane wood glues react with moisture in the wood and expand to fill any gaps. This can be useful if you have a loosely fitting blank, as the expansion will take up any slackness. The downside of this is that, as it cures, the glue can dislocate the tube in the blank or cause it to push out of the bore. Some form of clamping is advisable to prevent this. PU glue can also creep into the ends of the tubes, so plugging them with removable adhesive putty or modeling clay will avoid the need for later work clearing them out. Although it is less important with CA and epoxy, this technique can be used with those adhesives too.

A selection of adhesives for pen making.

Table of adhesive applications

	Cyanoacrylate	Polyurethane	Epoxy
Wood	✔	✔	✔
Stabilized wood	✔	✔	✔
Laminates	✔	✔	✔
Acrylics	✔	✗	✔
Clear cast	N/A	N/A	N/A
Solid surface material	✔	✗	✔
Polymer clay	N/A	N/A	N/A
Antler and horn	✔	✗	✔
Soapstone	✗	✗	✔

Epoxy

Epoxy glues consist of a resinous adhesive and a catalyst (hardener) **B** that must be mixed together **C** to create an adhesive. Working times can be from a few minutes to half an hour, and setting times vary from 10 minutes to 24 hours. Epoxies are more forgiving during assembly than CA and allow manipulation of the position of the tube before leaving to cure. Even with fast setting epoxies, I prefer to leave the blanks overnight to cure before beginning turning, to ensure that they are fully set. If you are keen to get the work onto the lathe, using epoxies can delay the work.

Cyanoacrylate (CA)

CA instant glue is the most frequently used adhesive for pen making **D** . It has the advantage that it dries almost immediately and cures in a few minutes, so work on the project can progress without delay. I prefer to use thick CA for gluing blanks, although this is not critical. When using CA, the blanks should be checked carefully for fit before gluing in the tubes. A tightly fitting blank can result in a half-inserted tube firmly glued in position. This is a problem from which it is difficult, if not impossible, to recover without destroying the blank. Although I have never had a problem with a CA glue joint failing, I prefer to use epoxy adhesives for all my high-end work with wooden blanks.

Technical **tip**

My preferences are for cyanoacrylate (CA) glue when using acrylics and other synthetic materials, epoxies for wood and most laser-cut and laminated blanks, and polyurethane glues only when I have a problem with a loose-fitting blank that requires the gap-filling properties it provides. If you need to get the job done quickly, CA is perfectly adequate for wooden blanks, too. When using laser-cut blanks, follow the manufacturer's instructions as to which adhesives to use.

Plating

The material with which the metal components of pen and pencil kits are plated and the thickness of the plating are important factors in determining not only the appearance but also the quality and longevity of the product.

Gold

Gold  is the most common plating and is usually available in either 10 carat or 24 carat. Neither is particularly hard wearing and 24 carat is particularly soft. As a result gold plating is most frequently used on the less expensive kits or the cheaper versions of mid-range kits. All gold plating will wear away through use eventually but the thicker the plating the longer it will last and some manufacturers also apply additional coatings of lacquer or epoxy to delay the process.

Some kits are described as having "upgrade gold" plating. This usually means that the parts are plated using small amounts of cobalt or palladium added to the plating chemicals to increase durability.

Rhodium

This is one of the most expensive of all the plating types and is a very durable metal closely related to platinum. Along with durability, rhodium offers good resistance to corrosion, tarnishing, and abrasion. It gives a finish similar in appearance to chrome plating but has better wearing properties and is used in some of the highest quality kits **B**. Some manufacturers use real platinum rather than rhodium, making their pens even more durable.

Titanium

Titanium plating is available in black (titanium oxide) **C** or gold (titanium nitride) and while it is less expensive than rhodium it has similar properties of wear and corrosion resistance. It offers a good compromise between the more expensive rhodium and the cheaper gold plating.

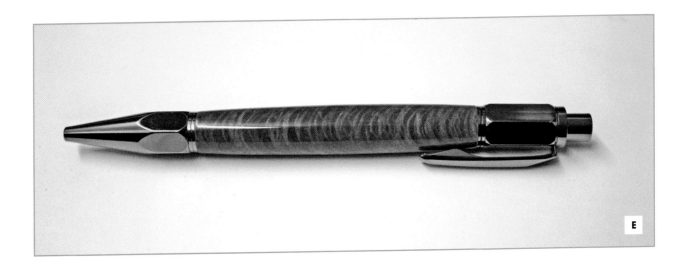

E

Chrome

Chrome plating **D** is another robust option and it is cheaper than the rhodium or titanium alternatives. Many woods and acrylics look good with a chrome colored plating, making it a popular choice. Black chrome is also available.

Copper

Copper is becoming more frequently used as plating for pens. Like gold, it is a soft metal, wears and scratches easily, and requires a protective coating of epoxy to make it last for a reasonable time.

Other alternatives

Other types of plating available include gunmetal **E** (a type of bronze that is reasonably resistant to wear and tends to give an antique look because of its darker color), Swiss Rose Gold (made from a mixture of gold and copper that is very durable, but rare and expensive), and sterling silver (fairly durable but is only occasionally used as plating for pen kits).

Finally, some cheaper kits are now available in colorful finishes with descriptions such as "metallic green." These are applied coatings rather than plating, and they have durability and wear qualities similar to painted or powder-coated surfaces.

Technical **tip**

I always try to match both the appearance and quality of the material I am using for pen barrels to the appearance and quality of the kit and its plating. An expensive burl or a complicated casting that I have spent hours or even days creating looks best when matched to a kit with fittings of commensurate quality. Likewise an expensive fountain pen kit with top notch plating will benefit from barrels of some distinction rather than a plain or nondescript wood.

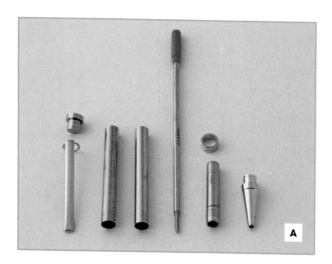

Pen and pencil kits

Although it is quite possible to make pens and pencils virtually from scratch by buying only the nib units or mechanisms and turning the rest of the components from metal, wood, or acrylic, most makers will create all of their pens using the many and varied kits that are available, while the more adventurous may create their own designs by modifying the kits.

The available kits vary in complexity from very simple single barrel pens to quite complex fountain pens with many components. Most are designed to be made by turning on a mandrel with bushings, although a few use alternative methods. In this section I will describe four kits that represent the basic styles available.

Slimline

Most beginners start out on their pen-making journey with the ubiquitous Slimline kit **A** . This is a relatively simple kit consisting of only eight components, and the process of making one is described in Project No. 1 (see p. 74). It is a good kit for beginners, as making it involves most of the basic processes required for pen making. Matching pencil kits are also available, and together they compose an attractive set that makes a relatively inexpensive gift or will sell well at craft fairs.

The Slimline kit also lends itself well to modification from the simple straight barrels that it is intended to have. A thickened grip tapering back through to the narrow center band and then broadening out again in an elegant sweep toward the end cap can look good, but do beware of the beginner's mistake of creating two fat barrels curving steeply toward the center band and looking like nothing more than a sack tied in the middle. If you want a fatter pen, better options are to buy the Streamline kit, which is similar but has a thicker center band, or to buy a broad center band to replace the narrow one. Another alternative, which discards the center band altogether, is described in Project No. 9 (see p. 110).

Sierra

Simple though the Slimline kit is, it is not the most basic of designs in terms of difficulty of making. The single barrel types, such as the Sierra **B** , require the making of only one barrel, have fewer components that require assembly, and present no issues of grain or pattern matching. Despite a small cost premium over the Slimline, the Sierra represents an easy way to make a more appealing pen, perhaps with better quality plating or to show off an attractive wooden or acrylic blank. This type of pen is also the preferred basis for most laser-cut kits and clear cast blanks. The making of a simple acrylic Sierra is described in Project No. 2 (see p. 80) and it is also used as the basis of several other projects.

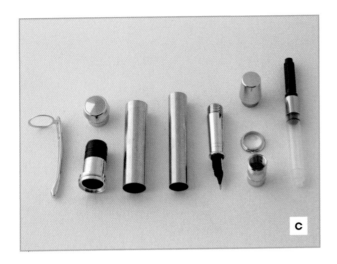

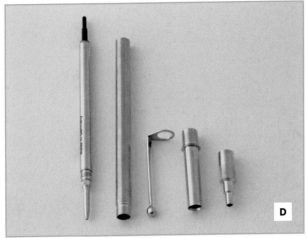

Junior Gentleman

Moving on in complexity, we come to the fountain pens and roller ball pens with two-part barrels and screw fittings. The basic design varies little from kit to kit, although the style and complexity of the components is much more variable. The Junior Gentleman's Pen **C**, also known as the Gentleman's Classic by some UK suppliers, is a typical example of the genre. It is used as the basis for the Burl Elm Fountain Pen described in Project No. 3 (see p 84).

dns-Twister

Finally there are some kits that vary from the standard mandrel and bushings form of making. These are turned between centers and require either the use of special fitments or the manufacture of shop-made devices to mount them on the lathe. The dns-Twister pen and pencil kits **D**, for example, are not complex in their number of components or design but require a greater degree of skill from the maker and provide an interesting challenge for those wishing to advance their skills. Without the constraint of center bands or other metal components, they also provide almost unlimited scope for design innovation.

From left to right: Slimline, Sierra, Junior Gentleman and dns-Twister.

CHAPTER TWO
TECHNIQUES

SAFETY

Like any other activity that involves the use of machinery or working with sharp tools, turning, and therefore pen making, is potentially dangerous. It is your responsibility to ensure your own safety and that of others who may be in the vicinity of your pen-making activities.

General guidance

This section is not intended to be a comprehensive manual of health and safety requirements for the workshop but is included to highlight some of the principal risks involved. You should also make sure that you have read and understood the safety instructions supplied with all of your tools and machinery and familiarized yourself with any local laws, regulations, or guidance related to relevant heath and safety issues. The guidance provided to ensure the safety of employees in commercial workshops is not usually legally binding upon individuals in their own premises, but the principles upon which it is based are sound and where appropriate it should be followed.

Always wear suitable clothing when working with lathes and other machinery—elasticized cuffs rather than loose sleeves, jewelry and neckties removed, long hair tied back or retained in suitable headgear. Never wear gloves when using woodworking machinery. A wood turning smock or woodworker's apron is a sensible investment.

Protect yourself

Face and eye protection are vital. I put on a pair of safety glasses **A** the moment I enter the workshop and keep them on at all times, supplementing them with a full face mask or respirator as necessary. Do not be deluded into thinking that because you are working with small workpieces you are safe from injury. A chip of wood flying off a 1-in.- (25-mm-) diameter pen blank revolving at 2,000 rpm will be traveling at about 9 ft. (3m) per second. You do not want to get your face in the way of something traveling at that speed, however small. And always remember, you are working with your last set of eyes.

A

Dust and fumes from adhesives and finishes are further hazards against which suitable precautions must be taken. Some woods are known to have toxic dust, but all particulates are potentially damaging if inhaled. Using an extractor with a suitably fine filter will remove the bulk of the dust, and adding an ambient air filter will also help, but the only way to ensure full protection from both dust and chemical fumes is to wear a suitably rated face mask or, better still, a powered respirator **B** .

Safe practice

Always make sure that your tools are sharp and that you know how to use them. Trying to force a blunt tool is unlikely to produce fine work and much more likely to result in an accident than using a sharp blade. Do make sure that you get suitable training before using wood turning tools. Improper use can result in catches and even broken tools, with potentially disastrous results. The guidance on tool technique given in this book is by its nature very basic and cannot substitute for instruction from a skilled turner. "If in doubt, find out" is a good maxim to apply before starting to use any tool or machine.

Finally, a word on chemicals such as stains, finishes, and adhesives. Always make sure these are stored safely in their original containers and away from children and other vulnerable people. Always read the instructions and safety data sheets, and be especially careful when using volatile or flammable substances. A workshop fire extinguisher of the dry powder type **C** is a good safety investment.

BLANK PREPARATION

Before beginning any work on the lathe, the blanks must be prepared for turning.
They will need to be cut to size, drilled to take the brass tubes, glued to the tubes,
and squared off to ensure a good fit to the other components of the pen or pencil.

Cutting

Ready prepared wooden pen blanks are available in a wide
range of wood species, but another option is to obtain offcuts
or pieces that are too small for other woodworkers to use and
to make your own blanks from these. This can often be cheaper
and also you have the option to try cross cutting or diagonal
cutting across the grain of the wood **A**, which can produce
interesting and varied patterns of figure in the finished pen or
pencil. Small pieces of burl that might otherwise be discarded
can also be used to create interesting pen blanks.

Whether you buy blanks or create your own, and whether
you are using wood or an alternative material, the blanks
will need to be cut to length to suit the kit you are using.

Before cutting, decide the orientation of the grain or pattern
that will give the best appearance in the finished pen and
draw a line with a marker pen along the blank, indicating
with an arrowhead which will be the nib end **B**. This will
enable you to keep the components aligned during the
making process. Mark to the length required for each part
of the pen using the brass tubes as a guide. Leave each blank
⅛ in. (3mm) to ¼ in. (6mm) longer than the tube to allow
for trimming later.

The actual cutting can be done either by hand using a tenon
saw and bench hook or with a powered bandsaw, tablesaw,
or miter saw. If using a powered saw be sure to use the
fences and guides to cut safely, and remember to cut off
any short waste pieces first to avoid the need to handle very
small components near the blade. Simple jigs can make the
process easier and safer. For example, for cutting blanks on
the bandsaw I have made a jig that can be adjusted to suit
the length of the tube **C**.

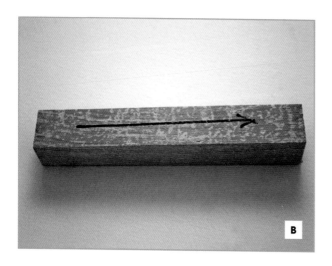

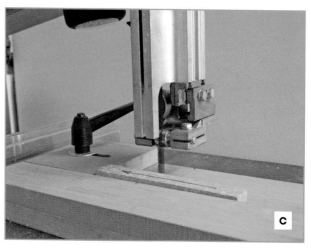

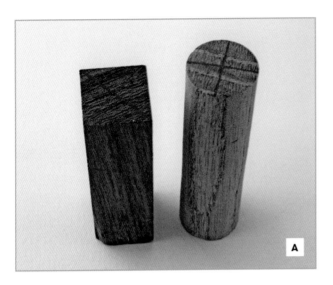

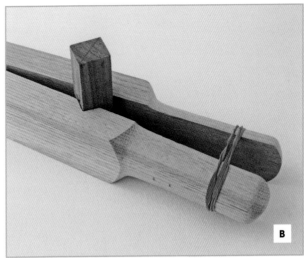

Drilling

A very important factor in ensuring a good quality pen is the bore in the prepared blank, which must be parallel and concentric. A blank with a bore that runs off-center may result in poor matching of the figure of the wood or the pattern of man-made materials. A hole that is not concentric, in other words one that appears oval when viewed from the end of the blank, will at best result in a poorly fitting tube (which may in turn cause an out-of-shape pen barrel) or at worst may make effective fitting and gluing of the tube difficult if not impossible. A little care taken at this preparatory stage can save much frustration later by preventing problems caused by ill-fitting tubes and can contribute to the quality of the finished work.

Drilling can be performed using a drill press or a power drill in a stand, or can be undertaken on the lathe. Either method can be effective and accurate, but each requires the blank to be held firmly in relation to the drill bit and the drill bit to be secured in an accurate and true-running chuck.

Before beginning to drill, it is advisable to mark the center of the end of the blank by drawing two diagonal lines from the corners of a square blank or using a center finder with a round one **A** . Starting to drill on center will mean that there is less chance of any runout that could result in a split or shattered blank. Also, with two-part pen kits, always begin to drill from the end of the blank that you have already marked to be in the middle of the pen or pencil, as this will ensure the best grain or pattern match.

When using a drill press or stand, the blank must always be held square to the drill bit. This can be achieved using a vise or cross vise, a homemade clamping device **B** , or a dedicated holding device **C** . When using a vise or cross vise, make sure that the blank is vertical by checking with a small engineering square **D** . If you do not have a small square, you can check for square by truing the blank against the drill bit.

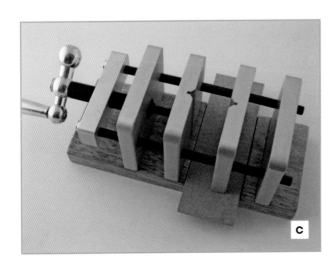

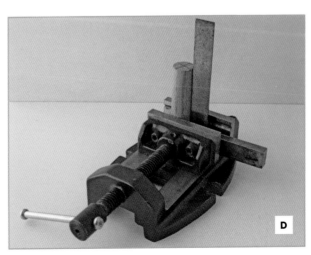

When drilling on the lathe, the blank should be mounted on the headstock in a chuck fitted with engineering jaws or pin jaws **E** or in a dedicated pen blank chuck **F**, while the drill bit should be held in the tailstock using a Jacobs chuck or collet chuck.

Whichever method is used, you should check carefully that you are using the correct size drill bit as recommended by the kit manufacturer, whether metric or imperial, as there is seldom an exact alternative. Drill at a slow speed and withdraw the drill bit regularly to remove shavings or swarf—drilling too fast or with the flutes of the bit blocked with waste material will cause the bit and the workpiece to overheat, damaging the drill bit and resulting in an inaccurate hole or breakout, or splitting of the blank. A small stiff-bristled brush will rapidly clear waste from the flutes. By following these procedures you should obtain a blank with a bore that is both parallel and concentric, and this will form the foundation of a fine pen or pencil.

Technical **tip**

When drilling acrylic blanks or thin wooden ones, chipping or splitting can occur as the drill bit breaks through the far end of the blank. This can be avoided by cutting the blank a little longer than required, drilling just short of breakthrough, and then cutting back the blank to the required length, leaving a clean hole. (Remember to leave the blank long enough for squaring the ends.)

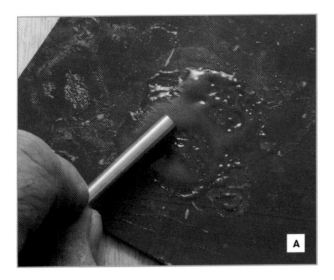

Gluing

Gluing the brass tubes into the prepared blanks is an important part of the pen and pencil making process. A poorly made glue joint can fail either during making or in use, resulting at best in wasted time and effort or at worst in a disappointed end user. Glue residues in the tube from careless work can cause poor fitting of the components or even cracking of the barrels on assembly.

To avoid these problems it is important to follow a careful process. This process is much the same whatever adhesive you use. First of all, check the fit of the tubes before applying any adhesive and correct if necessary so that they are a smooth sliding fit in the blanks. If the fit is too tight the blank may split, and if using CA the brass tube may jam irretrievably partway into the hole, rendering the blank useless and possibly destroying the tube. If the fit is too slack the tube may not seat correctly, causing misshapen barrels or poor component fit. If the holes are not concentric (i.e. they appear oval) and a good fit cannot be achieved it is better to discard the blank and start again, taking greater care with the drilling process next time, for if the tube does not fit correctly you will most likely end up with a misshapen barrel that does not fit the components properly.

Before applying adhesive, some makers seal the ends of the tubes to prevent glue ingress by pressing the end of the tube into modeling clay, putty, or even a potato. I prefer to simply take care to avoid using too much adhesive and to remove any that does get into the tube with the a rolled-up tissue or a cotton wool swab before it sets. If you decide to seal the tubes, which will keep them clear of glue for sure, then do this now before applying any adhesive.

Lightly sand the outside of the brass tube with fine aluminum oxide abrasive to remove any contaminants and provide a key for the adhesive.

Next, spread adhesive evenly over one half of the tube, either using a spatula or by rolling the tube in a pool of adhesive on a paper towel or other disposable surface **A** . Use the tube to spread the adhesive evenly on the inside of the drilled hole from each end (you will need to work quickly if using CA adhesive). Finally slide the brass tube, glued end first, into the drilled and glued hole. This will ensure that adhesive is spread evenly over the whole of the joint between the brass tube and the blank. Make sure the brass tube is fully inserted and pushed just 1/16 in. (2mm) inside the end of the blank to leave a little leeway for trimming **B** . At this stage I carefully check for and remove any surplus adhesive from inside the tubes.

Technical **tip**

Working with adhesives can be messy and with CA, which dries very quickly, there is a risk of things which are not meant to be joined becoming stuck together. This includes the possibility of gluing your fingers to the blanks or the glue pot. To avoid this I often wear latex gloves when using CA, either as an adhesive or as a finish.

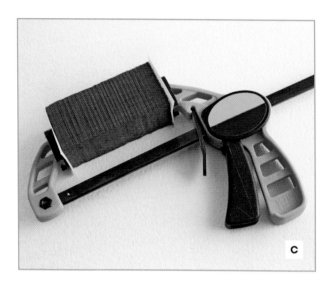

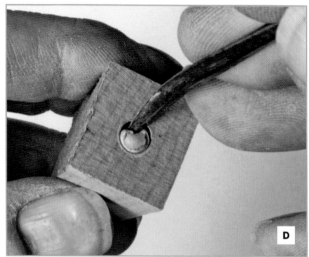

If you have used polyurethane adhesive, which expands as it cures, it is wise to place a cramp around the ends of the blank to prevent the adhesive from forcing the tube out of the hole as it sets. Make sure to use a barrier such as a paper towel or card between the cramp and the blank to avoid gluing them together **C**.

All that remains now before moving on to trimming is to leave the glue to set. For CA this may be only a few minutes; for epoxy or polyurethane glue I find it best to leave overnight. If you have sealed the tubes with modeling clay or an alternative this can be safely removed and discarded once the adhesive has set **D**.

Technical **tip**

The drying times of adhesives can vary considerably from brand to brand. Some epoxies, for example, will set in five to ten minutes, others will take thirty minutes to an hour, and yet others will need to be left overnight. Atmospheric conditions and temperature can also affect setting times so be sure to read and follow the manufacturers instructions carefully and make sure the tube is firmly set in the blank before beginning any further work.

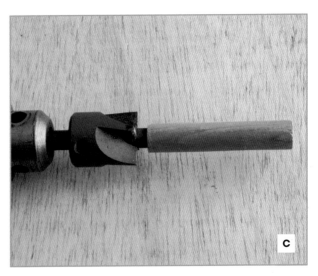

Trimming

Trimming the blanks is the final stage of preparation before mounting on the lathe and beginning to turn. It is done to ensure that the ends of the completed barrels are a good square fit to the metal components of the pen without unsightly gaps.

However carefully you have cut and drilled the blanks it is unlikely that the ends will be at absolutely 90° to the ends of the brass tubes. The slightest inaccuracy here will leave a visible gap but careful trimming will prevent this.

In trimming the blanks it is important to remember that you are squaring the ends of the barrel in relation to the brass tube and not to the blank itself. In order to do this, any jigs or tools must register with the brass tube. Simply squaring the end of a blank on a disk sander for example will not ensure a true barrel as the end will then be at right angles to the sides of the blank but not necessarily to the brass tube.

One simple way to ensure accuracy if using a disk sander is first to mount the blank on a mandrel in the lathe and turn it to a cylinder. The sides of the cylinder will then be parallel with the tube and when squared on the sander the ends will be true. A good alternative is to buy or make a jig designed to hold the blank by the brass tube and square to the disk **A** .

The most popular way of squaring the blanks is to use a barrel trimmer **B** . This can be used either manually, by fitting in a handle or in the tailstock, or under power in a drill press, lathe, or cordless power drill. If you use a power tool, the blank should be held firmly in a vise or, if using the lathe, with a clamp or other holding device.

A further consideration when using a barrel trimmer is that the diameter of the trimmer shaft should be as close as possible to the inside diameter of the tube. Trimming a large diameter blank with a small diameter shaft may result in an out-of-square barrel. Barrel trimmer shafts and sleeves are available to fit the majority of popular tube sizes or you can easily turn your own sleeve using a spare 7-mm tube fitted into a blank that is then turned down to fit the inside diameter of the tube **C** .

Holding Work on the Lathe

Before any turning work can begin the prepared blank or blanks must be mounted on the lathe. The most popular means of doing so is by the use of a mandrel and bushings, although some turners prefer to mount the blank in the bushings and the bushings between centers.

Mounting using a mandrel

While it may seem a simple matter to mount the prepared blanks and bushings on the mandrel, mount the mandrel on the lathe, and tighten up the tailstock, it is necessary to undertake this process with care and in the right order to ensure that everything runs true.

Begin by checking that your lathe headstock and tailstock are aligned properly. Check that the Morse tapers of the lathe are clean and free from contamination, insert a center into each Morse taper, and then bring the tailstock up until the points almost touch. When the lathe is turned by hand the points of the centers should remain aligned. If this is not the case then you will need to check the instructions for your lathe and correct the alignment. Mount the mandrel in the headstock Morse taper and then mount the bushings and blanks loosely on the mandrel shaft. Make sure the bushings are in the correct order as shown in the instructions for the kit you are using and that the blanks are aligned in accordance with any marking out that you used to ensure grain alignment. If using an adjustable mandrel, adjust the length to suit the blanks according to the instructions for your mandrel. If the mandrel is fixed, use packing pieces or spare bushings to take up any excess space before lightly screwing on the mandrel nut. Do not tighten the mandrel nut at this stage.

Now, with a revolving center fitted, bring up the tailstock until it nearly engages with the dimple in the end of the mandrel. Do not bring the tailstock up heavily against the mandrel as this can cause bending and misalignment, possible even permanently damaging the alignment of the mandrel. Wind the tailstock quill gently up to the mandrel, tightening just enough for the revolving center to turn without slipping when the lathe is turned by hand. The purpose of the tailstock is only to hold the mandrel in the

A

headstock and to maintain alignment. Overtightening is not necessary and, as well as causing misalignment, may damage the bearings in the live center or headstock.

Finally, tighten the mandrel nut by hand until the blanks and bushings are held firmly in place sufficiently tightly for them not to revolve on the mandrel when cutting pressure is applied from the tools. Again, overtightening can cause misalignment so take care not to overdo it at this stage; you can always tighten them a bit more if there is any slipping. Your blanks are now ready to begin turning **A**.

Technical **tip**

The proper mounting of the work is important in ensuring the accuracy of the shape and fit of the finished pen. Misalignment or over- or under-tightening of mandrel nuts or tailstock can result in runout that will mean the finished barrels are not concentric or have a poor fit with the components.

Mounting between centers

Mounting between centers is the preferred method of many pen makers as it eliminates any inaccuracy or runout arising from a misaligned mandrel. This method requires that the bushings fit into the ends of the tubes so it will not work with standard 10-mm bushings.

To use this method the bushings are inserted into the ends of the prepared blanks and then mounted in the lathe between a 60° dead center in the headstock and a 60° live center in the tailstock. The tailstock is then tightened sufficiently for the blank to resist the cutting pressure of the tool without slipping. This method of work holding also works well when finishing with cyanoacrylate. By removing the bushings and placing the barrel directly between centers **B** the ends of the barrel are not in contact with either bushings or centers and the problem of bushings becoming glued to the barrel is avoided. There is a slight risk with this method of work holding that if too much pressure is applied with the tailstock by over tightening, flaring of the ends of the brass tubes will result causing poor fit of the components, or worse still a cracked blank destroying all your work so far. Tightening the tailstock only enough to enable the finish to be applied and polished will avoid these potential problems.

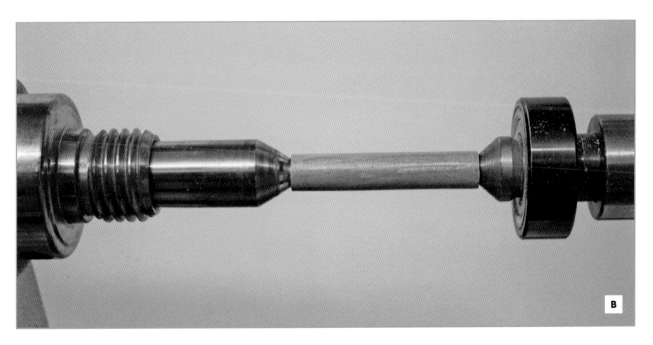

B

Turning

Many readers will already be skilled in the use of wood-turning tools and it is beyond the scope of this book to provide comprehensive instruction on basic tool technique. The best way to learn is from a skilled turner, perhaps from a professional or through membership of a wood-turning club. The next three sections explain, largely for the benefit of the beginner, how the spindle roughing gouge, skew chisel, and scraping tools are used in relation to the turning of pens and how to make the basic cuts needed.

General tool use considerations

Before beginning to explain the basic tool techniques that I use for pen making it is perhaps worth reminding readers, especially those who are beginners to wood turning, that there are perhaps as many different opinions of what is and is not correct tool technique as there are wood turners. There is little agreement on what tool to use or how to use it and provided that the methods used are safe there is, in my opinion, no wrong way of working.

Of one thing I am sure, however, and that is that there is no harder way to learn how to use your tools than to try to do so from reading a book such as this. Observing what works for others and copying or adapting their techniques is a much better way to learn, and this can easily be done by taking a class, joining a club, or watching some of the many video demonstrations that are available online or on DVD.

The techniques that I describe here are the ones that work for me, and although I explain the use of various tools, in reality I undertake the vast majority of my pen turning with a spindle roughing gouge, using it variously as a gouge, a skew chisel, and a scraper. I have, however, refined the methods described here over many years and they are what I would recommend for beginners. As you develop your tool skills you will also develop your own preferred ways of working and if it works for you that is all that matters.

Spindle roughing gouge

The spindle roughing gouge is the first tool that most turners will experience. Its primary role, as its name suggests, is in spindle work for turning square or rough stock to a cylinder. For the purposes of pen making it is used to turn the prepared blanks down almost to size before using a skew chisel to undertake the final finishing cuts. Before beginning work make sure that your gouge is sharp and that you are wearing appropriate safety equipment. Goggles or safety glasses are essential and full face protection is even better.

Begin by placing the tool firmly on the rest, square to the work with the handle pointing downward **A** . Bring the tool into contact with the work so the bevel is rubbing **B** .

Raise the handle until the tool begins to cut, then move the gouge along the work in the direction of the cut, turning the tool so the flute of the gouge is facing in the direction of the cut and the cut is made with the wing of the gouge. Take care to keep the wing tips out of contact **C** . Continue to make cuts in this way until the blanks have been turned down to just a few fractions of an inch (several millimeters) larger than the bushings.

Technical **tip**

Take light cuts to ensure a clean surface. If the blank shows signs of tearout (or splintering if you are using acrylics), the cuts you are taking may be too heavy or your gouge may not be sharp enough. Sharp tools and light cuts are vital to good pen making.

Once you have smooth cylindrical blanks it is time to move on to the finishing cuts using the skew chisel, but it is also possible to use the spindle roughing gouge for the finishing cuts by skewing the gouge slightly to one side to take a shearing cut **D** . I often use this technique to save time changing tools when making production runs.

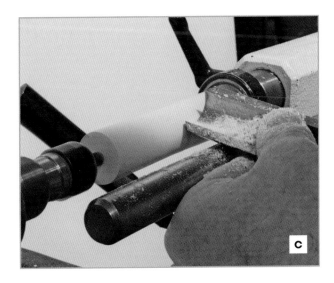

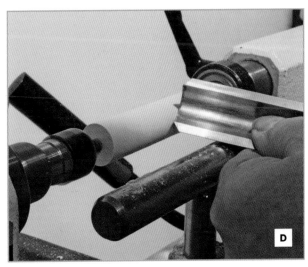

Skew chisel

Many turners shy away from the skew chisel either because they have had a bad experience of dig-ins caused by poor presentation of the tool to the work or because they have been mistakenly advised that it is a difficult or dangerous tool to use. This is a great pity, because with a little practice and proper use, the skew is one of the most handy and versatile tools a wood turner can possess.

A skew chisel is undoubtedly the best tool to use if you wish to achieve a fine finish on pen barrels and other spindle work. It can also be used for the cutting of beads and chamfers, parting off work, and shaping the dovetails for bowl spigots. It also makes an excellent negative rake scraper and much more besides. However, for the purposes of pen making all that we need to know is how to make a simple planing or smoothing cut. The method described here is the "heel down" technique.

Begin by placing the tool firmly on the rest (which should be placed slightly above center height) with the handle at right angles to the axis of the lathe and pointing slightly downward. Bring the tool into contact with the work so the bevel is rubbing **A** . Make sure that only the bevel in the middle of the tool is in contact with the work and that neither of the points comes into contact.

Twist the handle in the direction of the cut until the tool begins to cut then move the tool along the work in the direction of the cut. Keep the cut to the lower half of the cutting edge avoiding the point **B** . As with the roughing gouge, take light cuts to ensure a good clean surface.

The skew chisel may also be used as a negative rake scraper. It should be held firmly on the rest and horizontal to the work, and in this position it can be used to make light finishing cuts that are particularly useful when working with acrylics **C** .

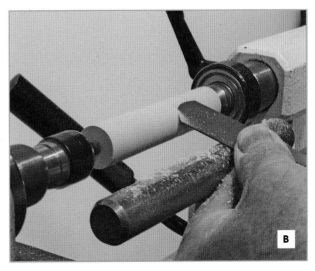

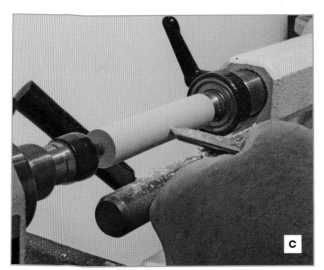

Scrapers

The long held myth that scrapers are not "proper" wood turning tools is, I'm thankful to say, gradually being dispelled. It is my view that any tool that can be used to achieve the desired result effectively and safely is appropriate.

The accepted wisdom is that scrapers should be sharpened in a similar way to the cabinet scrapers used by furniture makers, with a raised burr on the cutting edge of the tool. I do not find this to be an effective way of using scrapers to achieve a fine finish in pen making. Rather than raising a burr, I sharpen my scrapers by polishing the flat face of the tool with a diamond hone or waterstone and present the tool with the flat surface at 90° to the work to take a fine shearing cut **D** . With a light touch this will produce an almost polished finish, especially on very hard woods and acrylic materials. Care is needed with this method, however, as too much pressure can introduce stresses that will cause tearout in wood or splintering of acrylics.

Spindlemaster

The Spindlemaster was designed to overcome the problems that some turners experience with a skew chisel. Because it has no points to dig in, its use is very straightforward and it will produce a surface almost as fine as with the skew. Like the skew, it can be used either to make a planing cut or as a scraping tool. To make a planing cut, place the tool rest at or below center height and place the tool firmly on the rest (flat surface uppermost) with the handle pointing down. Bring the bevel into contact with the work **A** .

Raise the handle slowly until the tool begins to cut, then twist the handle slightly and move in the direction of the cut **B** .

To use the Spindlemaster as a scraper, the tool rest should be placed on center height. With the handle at right angles to the axis of the lathe and horizontal bring the tool up to the work until it begins to take a light cut then slide along the tool rest in the direction of the cut **C** .

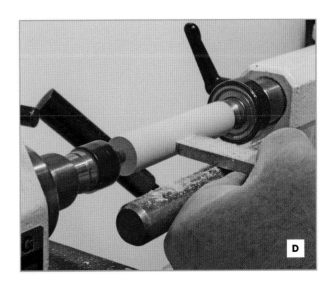

POLYMER CLAY

Polymer clay is an extremely versatile medium and the options for its use in pen making are limited only by the imagination of the pen maker. The material is available in packs of colored clays , ready-made millefiori canes, or even as finished blanks that only require turning to shape, so how you use it is an individual choice.

Mix and match

The raw material must be worked to soften it before using to create pen barrels, and the various colors can be mixed or even used with other materials such as acrylic paints and other craft materials. Once shaped, either from the raw material or by using millefiori canes as shown in Project No. 8 (see p. 104), the completed barrels must be baked in a stove to harden the material and prepare the barrel for final finishing. The baked material can be worked with most woodworking tools and can be carved, sawn, sanded, or turned on the lathe.

Polymer clay is nontoxic but should not be used in conjunction with food items. Kitchen tools such as the pasta machine used in Project No. 8 can be very useful for polymer clay work, but once used with the clay they must never be used for food preparation again.

CASTING

Casting your own clear-cast or acrylic blanks is a great way to give your pens individuality and show off your creative ability. Polyester resin can be used to create clear-cast blanks or combined with pigments and other materials to create acrylic blanks every bit as attractive as those you can buy.

Clear casting

You can use clear casting to create a blank from almost anything that can be painted onto, glued to, or wrapped around a brass pen barrel. You may choose to use acrylic paints to decorate the barrel with a camouflage pattern or some artwork, attach feathers as if making a fishing fly, cover the tubes with attractive postage stamps or other printed material, or glue on other small items. Whatever you choose, be sure to cover the whole tube or paint it with a background color to avoid unsightly gaps.

Once you have prepared your tubes, the method of creating a clear-cast pen blank is the same whatever decoration you have used and is completed in three stages. As well as the resin and catalyst (hardener), you will need a mold for the blank, a disposable container in which to mix the resin and catalyst, and lollipop sticks and cocktail sticks for mixing and removing air bubbles. You will also require lead shot to weight the tubes, and cork or rubber bungs to seal the tubes. Kits are available containing all the equipment and materials necessary 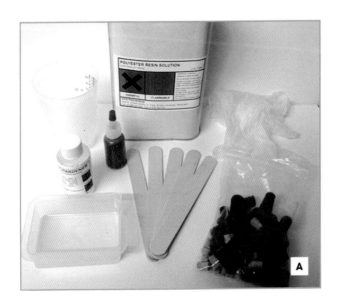 and these are a good investment when starting out with clear casting.

Begin by mixing together sufficient resin and hardener to create a base layer in the bottom of the mold about ¼ in. (6mm) thick. Mix the two components in the proportions recommended by the manufacturer. Pour the resin carefully into the mold and try to avoid creating any air bubbles. Any bubbles that do occur can be carefully removed using a toothpick. Leave overnight to harden. Once the base layer is set, the decorated tube (or tubes, if you choose to make more than one) must be weighted with lead shot and its ends sealed with cork or rubber bungs. It can then be carefully positioned in the mold. Mix up another batch of resin, just sufficient to cover the tube, and pour carefully into the mold 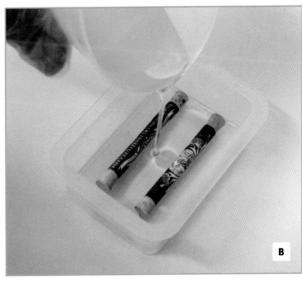, once

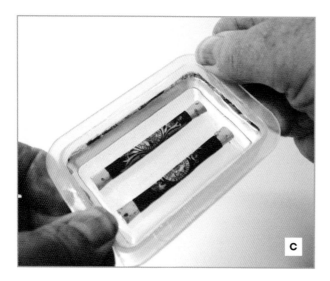

again taking care to remove any air bubbles that occur. This must then be set aside once again to harden overnight before pouring a final mix to fill up the mold.

When the whole assembly is finally set, the blank can be snapped out of the mold by twisting **C** or tapping on the bench and the ends trimmed away to remove the bungs and weights **D** . The ends can now be squared off and the completed blank mounted on the lathe for turning to fit your chosen pen kit.

Polyester resin blanks

Many turners will already have used colored polyester resin in the form of the InLace-type materials that can be used to create decorative inlays for a wide range of turned items. It is possible to make your own pen blanks from these materials, and you may want to experiment with this to start with, but if you intend to make pen blanks in any quantity this is an expensive option.

Polyester resin can be mixed with colored pigments and dyes, metal powders, and similar artists' materials to create colorful and varied blanks. All of the necessary materials are available from art and craft suppliers, and include opalescent, pearlescent, and metallic materials.

To make your own blanks you will need a mold of a suitable size for the number of blanks you intend to make, as well as containers and mixing equipment similar to that needed for clear casting.

In a suitable container, measure and mix up sufficient resin and catalyst to almost fill your mold and mix thoroughly, once again avoiding introducing air bubbles. When it is thoroughly mixed, introduce sufficient dye or pigment to the mix to ensure that the blanks will be opaque when finished. Combining more than one pigment or adding metal powders or pearlescent materials will enable you to produce an endless variety of swirling patterns. Pour the mix into the mold and continue stirring until you are happy with the appearance. Do not continue to stir after the mix has started to gel. Put it aside to set completely overnight and then remove from the mold as for clear casting. The finished work can then be cut up into individual blanks on the bandsaw and is ready to be worked just like bought-in acrylics.

SANDING AND POLISHING

Sanding is the final part of the process of preparing the pen barrel before applying a finish or polishing. Polishing is a finishing process and is carried out on man-made materials, stabilized blanks, some natural materials (such as bone and horn), and on CA finishes applied to other materials. It is included here as the process involves the use of abrasives and is carried out in much the same way as sanding.

Sanding

The amount of sanding required and the coarseness of the grit with which you begin the process will depend upon the quality of your tool work. If you have achieved a fine surface you may be able to start from as high as 320- or even 400-grit abrasive, but don't worry if you have to start as low as 120-grit. The important thing is that any unevenness, tearout, and other imperfections are removed.

Always leave the blank a fraction oversize to allow for the sanding process. How much to leave is something that you will learn only from experience as it will depend upon the amount of sanding you need to do, and this in turn will depend upon the quality of finish you have achieved with the tools. Sanding should be carried out with the lathe running at a slow speed. It is tempting to turn the lathe

speed up in an effort to speed up the process, but this is a mistake. Too high a speed will result in the abrasive and the workpiece overheating and this can, at worst, result in cracking of a wooden blank or melting of man-made materials. I generally sand at about 500 rpm, turning the speed up just a little for finer grits and micromesh abrasives.

Begin by sanding with the finest grit that you think will effectively remove any imperfections. Use only light pressure, as pressing too hard will reduce the efficiency of the abrasive, make it more likely to overheat, and encourage clogging. Start with the lathe running, moving the abrasive from side to side. Hold the abrasive lightly, sand from underneath the revolving blank **A**, and do not wrap the abrasive around your fingers. In this way, if the abrasive catches the work, it will

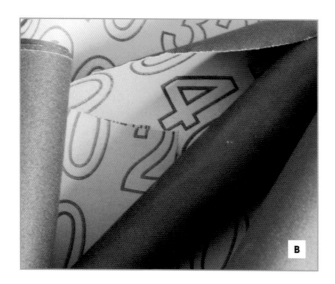

B

C

be harmlessly pulled away from you and you will not risk injury. Color Grit abrasives **B**, which are color coded and have the grit number printed on the backing material, or other cloth-backed abrasives **C** will last much longer than paper-backed types and will also be less prone to tearing. Stop the lathe regularly to check the surface, and once it seems all the imperfections have been removed sand lightly along the length of the blank with the lathe stationary to remove any circular marks.

Once you are happy with the surface, brush away any sanding dust and abrasive particles before repeating the process with the next grit. With wooden blanks it is advantageous to apply a thin coat of sanding sealer between each grit. This is especially important with blanks that use multiple wood species (e.g. laminated work) to avoid discoloration from contrasting sawdust contaminating the grain. Assuming you have started with a 120-grit abrasive, the progression is then 180, 240, 320, and 400. For wooden blanks you should not need to go beyond 400-grit; for acrylics, when you have reached 400-grit it is time to move on to polishing with micromesh abrasives.

It is important to remember that all marks from the tools, any tearout, or other irregularities must be removed with the coarsest grit of abrasive. The purpose of the finer grits is to remove the scratch pattern from the previous grit, nothing more. If defects have not been removed by the coarser abrasive, then the finer one is not going to remove them either. Sometimes defects that were not apparent after using the coarsest grit can reappear once the finer grits are used. Do not waste time attempting to remove them with the finer grit; go back to the coarse grit and repeat the whole process. This may sound like a lot of work but, trust me, it will save you a great deal of time and frustration.

Technical **tip**

Sanding is a vital part of pen making. Done properly it should leave the finished barrel smooth and free from blemishes and a perfect fit to the components of the pen or pencil. Done badly it can leave marks that mar the finished pen, reduce the barrel diameter so it is a poor fit, or even damage the blank to such an extent that it is not fit for use.

D

Polishing

Acrylic and other man-made materials, stabilized wood, colored laminated wooden blanks, and natural materials such as bone and horn can be brought to a finish by polishing. Polishing is also required to bring a CA finish to a high gloss. This section explains the use of micromesh abrasives for polishing on the lathe. The use of buffing compounds and mop wheels is covered in the section on buffing (see p. 77).

Micromesh abrasives start at about 1,500-grit and go up to 12,000-grit **D** . A typical range would be 1,500; 1,800; 2,400; 3,200; 3,600; 4,000; 6,000; 8,000; and 12,000. The finest grits produce a scratch pattern that is invisible to the human eye leaving a high gloss surface.

As with normal sanding, the process is to work through the grits of abrasive. Depending upon the material, it may not be necessary to use all the grits but to select a range of three or four, perhaps 1,500; 3,600; 6,000; and 12,000. Use a similar technique to that used for sanding, polishing first with the lathe running at about 1,500 to 1,800 rpm and then along the length of the blank with the lathe stationary.

Only a light touch is required. Remember, you are only polishing the surface. You do not need to remove a lot of material. Wipe away any dust and debris between grits and continue through the grits until you achieve the desired degree of shine.

Micromesh abrasives can be used either wet or dry. If using them wet take care to protect your lathe from water damage with rags or towels and wipe away the slurry created between grits with a damp cloth.

When polishing a CA finish, take care not to polish right through the finish to the substrate material. The abrasive only needs to be applied for a very short time to create an even scratch pattern on the surface before moving on to the next grit. If there is a defect in the finish of the substrate, no amount of polishing the finish will remove or conceal it. Similarly, defects in acrylics that have not been properly removed by the sanding process will never be completely removed by polishing alone.

FINISHING

The final stage before assembly is finishing of the barrels. Wooden barrels require an applied finish in order to achieve the degree of shine desired and to protect the surface from dirt and other contaminants that come from everyday handling of the pen or pencil; acrylics need only to be polished to the level of gloss required.

Choosing your finish

The type of finish preferred will depend upon the nature of the substrate and the degree of shine desired; there is no one finish that is suitable for all situations. The ideal finish would be highly durable, easy to apply to both smooth and textured surfaces, capable of creating any type of surface appearance from matte through to high gloss, and resistant to fingerprints. As far as I am aware no such ideal exists, even though pen makers have been searching for such a finish for many years. Nevertheless, despite the absence of a universal finish suitable for all situations, it is possible to achieve an excellent finish on all types of material by selecting the most appropriate finish for the material you have used to make the pen or pencil.

The chemical content of finishes will vary not only between different types of product but also between different manufacturers. Do take care to read any instructions or safety warnings provided by the supplier, either printed on the packaging or in product safety data sheets.

In the following sections, I will explain how various finishes are best used to achieve the highest-quality results. In the final section, I will also cover the use of abrasive compounds for the polishing of acrylics.

Friction polish

Friction polishes consist of a mixture of shellac and waxes dissolved in a solvent such as butanol, denatured alcohol, or white spirit, the exact composition varying considerably between brands. The solvent evaporates as a result of the application of friction, leaving the shellac and waxes to form a surface similar to that achieved with a traditional French polish. The very high gloss that can be achieved will have a high impact resistance but will lack durability unless protected with a coat of microcrystalline wax.

Friction polish is best applied to a smooth surface. It does not work well with textured surfaces or on barrels that have had a pattern worked on them with a Pen Wizard or similar ornamental device.

While it is not absolutely necessary to seal the surface of the wood before applying friction polish, I prefer to use a sanding sealer first. It does not really matter whether this is a cellulose- or shellac-based sealer (my own preference being for cellulose), but it is theoretically possible for the friction polish to react with an incompatible sealer, so if in any doubt use one that has a similar chemical base to the polish. Product instructions or data sheets will help in selecting compatible products. I apply a thin coat of sealer with a paintbrush, leave to dry, and then lightly sand with 400-grit abrasive or a Scotch Brite pad before applying the polish. An alternative is to apply the sealer with a cloth or paper towel while the lathe is running.

Lacquers

Acrylic and cellulose lacquers are available in liquid form and as aerosol sprays and can be used to finish pen and pencil barrels, either by direct application on the lathe or by spraying the barrels after removing them from the lathe. These lacquers can form a durable surface on both smooth and textured surfaces with careful application. Smooth surfaces are suitable for either on-lathe application or spraying. Textured surfaces should be spray-finished for the best results.

To apply the friction polish, apply a small amount of the polish to a cloth pad or a paper towel. With the lathe still, spread the polish over the pen barrel. Then, with the lathe running at about 1,000 rpm, apply an even, light pressure to the work with the still-damp pad, moving continuously from side to side until the base solvent evaporates and the shellac forms a high level of shine. If it is necessary, two or three applications of the polish can be made, following exactly the same process as before.

Appling too much polish, or using excessive lathe speed or pressure are the main causes of problems with this type of finish. While heat from the friction is necessary for the evaporation of the solvents, too much heat will cause the surface to melt, leaving ridges or, in the worst case, pieces of paper towel firmly stuck to the work. The best way to resolve these problems is by completely removing the polish with a suitable solvent or by sanding and then starting again using a lower lathe speed and/or less pressure.

Remember that using cloths with a rotating lathe is potentially very dangerous and can cause serious injury if the cloth becomes caught up in the work and drags your fingers in with it. To prevent this from happening, it is best to form the cloth into a pad and to hold this beneath the work so that the work is moving away from you **A** and the pad will be pulled safely away from your fingers in the event of a catch. Under no circumstances should you wrap the cloth around your fingers. Using paper towels or nonwoven pads that will tear if caught up in the moving work is an even safer option.

As with friction polishes, for finishing on the lathe I prefer to seal the barrels first with a sanding sealer. With these finishes it is even more important to match the sealer to the finishing product to avoid problems caused by the interaction of incompatible chemicals. Apply the lacquer using a cloth or paper pad with the lathe running. Speed of application is important as the solvents used in these products are volatile and consequently the lacquers dry very quickly. Wipe the product quickly over the surface, trying to achieve an even finish, and as soon as the surface is covered leave it to dry before applying further coats. Drying times will vary, but should be specified on the packaging or in the product data sheet.

Spraying is best carried out in a well-ventilated area and you may even want to wear some respiratory protection if you are going to do a lot of spraying. To avoid getting overspray everywhere I place the parts in a homemade spray booth made from a cardboard carton. You will also need to find a suitable way of holding the barrels for spraying. I find

this simple jig **B** , which is nothing more than an offcut with a couple of screws inserted, to be very effective. Spray by holding the can at the distance from the workpiece recommended by the product manufacturer and applying several light coats. Whichever method of application is used, lacquer finishes may require a final buffing once completely hardened to achieve a fine finish.

Cyanoacrylate (CA)

Cyanoacrylate instant glue has, over recent years, become the preferred finish of many pen makers. It undoubtedly provides the most durable surface and, as it is an acrylic compound, it can bring wooden pens and pencils to the same high gloss that can be achieved with acrylic materials. I must admit that I did at first have some reservations about using it, not least because to my tidy (some might say obsessive) mind, the use of an adhesive as a finish is just a little perverse. I also find the fumes offensive and its tendency to stick things together that were not intended to be stuck together is a little tedious. Despite these objections, I now use a CA finish for all of my mid-range and top end pens as there is, in my opinion, no better finish currently available. CA is, however, only suitable as a finish on smooth surfaces, as the method of application does not lend itself to textured or patterned barrels.

There are two main schools of thought regarding the method of application. Some makers prefer to use CA along with boiled linseed oil (BLO) while others prefer to use CA alone. I am of the opinion that BLO adds nothing to the process other than as a means of highlighting the figure of the wood before applying the CA, but I will describe both methods and you can decide for yourself which you prefer. By searching the Internet you will find many short videos demonstrating both methods, and you may find watching some of these a useful additional resource to use along with my descriptions. Whichever method you choose, you may want to consider wearing disposable vinyl or latex gloves and you must ensure adequate ventilation of the workspace. I use my dust collector to draw the fumes away and I also wear a powered respirator.

CA and linseed oil

To use the CA/BLO method, begin with a blank that has been sanded smooth and wiped clean with a rag or paper towel dampened with a solvent such as methylated spirit (denatured alcohol), methyl hydrate (wood alcohol/methanol), or cellulose thinners to remove any trace of grease or other contaminants. Open-grained wood is best sealed with a sanding sealer during the sanding process to fill any open pores, but the surface of the stock must be sanded back to bare wood to enable the BLO to penetrate the surface. With the lathe running at about 500 rpm, wipe the surface of the barrel with a thin coat of BLO to highlight the grain. Then fold a paper towel to form a long pad and apply a few drops of BLO to dampen it. Now apply three or four drops of CA onto the dampened section of towel. Holding the towel under the work (in a manner similar to that described for friction polish), apply the CA with a side-to-side motion and continue applying light pressure for a few seconds until a shine appears on the surface. Allow to dry for a few moments and then repeat the process. Three applications should prove

C

sufficient, although I have known of makers who apply as many as ten or fifteen. Continue until you are satisfied with the appearance of the surface. Once you are accomplished at the process you may find that all your barrels now need is polishing with a plastic polish or buffing with white diamond to achieve a high gloss. At first, however, you may find that spirals or ridges form in the surface of the finish and it will be necessary to polish these out using micromesh abrasives before applying further coats or final buffing.

CA on its own

The CA-only method may be used over a coat of BLO applied as in the initial step of the CA/BLO method or over a surface sealed with cellulose or acrylic sanding sealer. To apply the finish, form a paper towel pad a little wider than that for the CA/BLO method and run a thin line of CA onto the pad **C** . With the lathe running at about 500 rpm, apply the CA with a side-to-side motion, continuing only until an even application is achieved across the blank. Leave to dry before repeating the process as many times as you find necessary to achieve an acceptable finish. Some makers use CA accelerator to speed up the drying process between coats but I find that having the patience to wait for a few minutes between coats produces better results. Again, experiment with what works best for you. Many things, including the temperature and humidity of your climate, can cause your preferences to differ from mine. Final polishing and buffing are carried out in exactly the same way as for the CA/BLO method.

Buffing

Buffing can be used to bring acrylic, natural materials, and items that have been finished with CA or hard lacquers to a high gloss, or it can be used as a means of finishing textured work where an applied finish is not appropriate. Buffing should not be attempted on open-grained woods that have not been sealed, as compound will enter the open grain and cause staining that will be impossible to remove. A wide range of compounds, including Tripoli, white diamond, and carnauba wax **D** , is available for polishing all sorts of materials, and manufacturers' Web sites provide useful guidance on usage.

Buffing compounds are applied using mop wheels of varying hardness—harder for the coarser compounds ranging to very soft for finishing waxes. The effective hardness of the mop

D

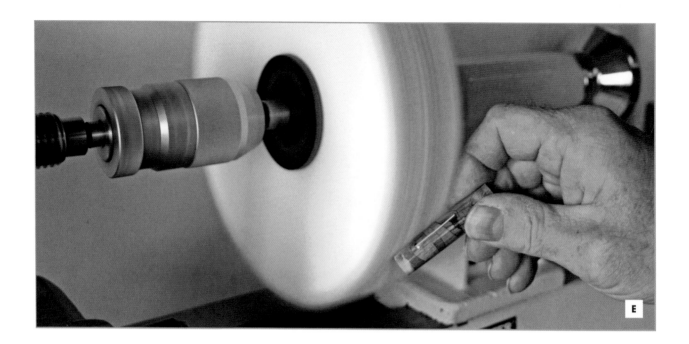

wheel also varies proportionately to the speed of rotation; the faster the speed, the harder the mop will be. I find speeds of 1,000 to 1,500 rpm are suitable for most purposes. Each mop wheel should be reserved for use with only one type of compound.

A good setup that will cover most situations is a firm wheel for Tripoli compound, a medium wheel for white diamond compound, and a soft wheel for carnauba wax. Kits are available containing all of these wheels and compounds, along with lathe mounting kits. These are ideal as starter kits but I find it cheaper to buy the wheels and compounds from specialty suppliers who can also supply the standard "pigtail" fittings required to mount the mop wheels in a chuck. Buffing should always begin with the coarsest compound required to remove the scratch pattern from previous finishing and work through to the finest compound or polish **E** .

Technical **tip**

Buffing wheels can be dangerous! The work must only be applied to the area of the buffing wheel that is rotating away from the work. You should ensure that you are aware where the safe area is to avoid a potentially serious accident. Objects thrown away from a buffing wheel will be traveling at high speeds. Always wear safety glasses and a dust mask when buffing.

ASSEMBLY

Now that you have prepared, turned, sanded, and finished your blanks, all that remains is to assemble the completed barrels with the rest of the pen or pencil components. It can be tempting to think that this is a simple matter of pressing the components into the brass tubes, but a little carelessness can result in disaster even at this stage, so taking a little time to prepare properly will pay dividends. In this section I will set out the procedure that I follow and then talk about disassembly if repairs are needed or if something has gone wrong.

Getting organized

The first and most important step is to set out all the components for assembly in the correct order. The instructions supplied with the kit should help here, but if these were not included then many of the major distributors of pen kits have detailed instructions available on their Web sites for the kits that they market. Making sure that all the pieces are fitted, and that they are fitted in the right position and in the right order, will preclude the frustration of finding that you have assembled the whole thing and left off the clip or a trim ring from a center band.

Check and press

Before beginning to press the components into the ends of the brass tubes, have a last check to ensure that all traces of adhesive have been removed and that the ends of the barrels are clean and free from anything that would prevent the parts from seating properly. If necessary, remove any adhesive residues with a sharp craft knife.

The components can now be pressed into the tube using a proprietary pen press **A**, although to me this seems an unnecessarily expensive piece of equipment to purchase

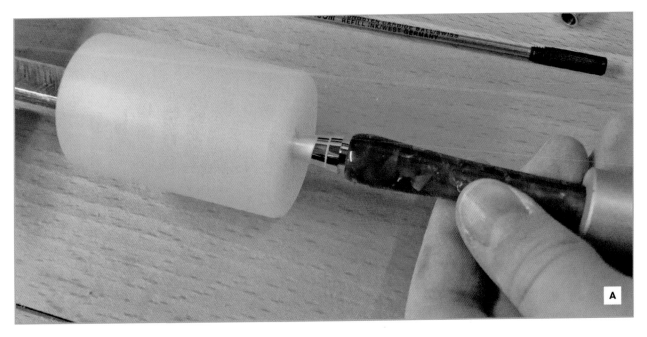

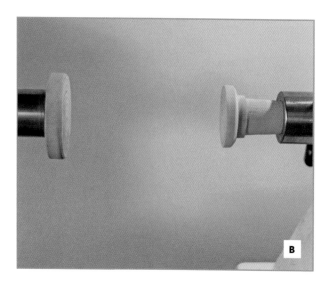

when you already have a lathe with a head and tailstock that can do the job and most likely a bench vise or drill press that can be used to equally good effect. I have made up wooden inserts for my head and tailstocks **B** and use the tailstock quill as a press.

The ends of the screw threads on some components can be delicate and easily damaged, so often it is wise to use a tube or spare bushing to protect the component when pressing into the tube **C** . Also look out for projecting parts of clips etc. that may be damaged by the jaws of whatever pressing device you are using.

It is also a good idea to ensure that the clip does not scratch or damage the finish of the barrel as it is pressed in. You can achieve this by sliding a suitable piece of plastic tubing over the end of the clip **D** .

Should you subsequently need to disassemble your pen or pencil, this can be achieved by carefully drifting out the components with a suitably sized transfer punch **E** . To disassemble a Slimline pen, for example, you will need first to use a narrow punch passed through the mechanism all the way to the tip, which is then tapped out with a few light hammer blows to the punch. A broader punch, as wide as will fit the tube, is then inserted from the other end and used to tap out the mechanism. Special care is needed not to damage plastic mechanisms, and the exact method of working will vary depending upon the style of the kit you are working on.

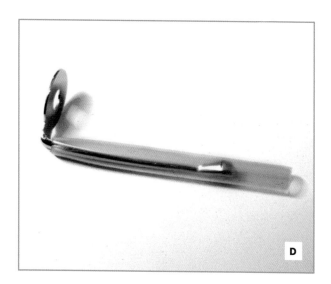

Parts of a typical fountain pen

Nib unit

Barrel coupler

End cap

Clip

Barrel tube

Ink pump mechanism

Cap tube

Barrel end cap

Cap center coupler

CHAPTER THREE
PROJECTS

TEAK SLIMLINE PEN

The Slimline pen is the kit that most beginners will encounter when they come to make their first pen. It is supplied with most starter packs as it is a relatively easy pen to make, and it is also an ideal project to use as a basis to explain all of the basic techniques required for pen making. For this project I have chosen to use the simplest methods and the most basic equipment, but many of the alternatives explained in Chapter 2 can be used instead.

Tools and materials

Slimline Pen kit

Type-A (7-mm) mandrel and standard 7-mm bushings

7-mm drill bit

Teak blank 6 in. (150mm) long

Barrel trimmer

Roughing gouge and skew chisel

CA adhesive

240-, 320-, and 400-grit aluminum oxide abrasive

Cellulose sanding sealer

Friction polish

Step 1 Begin by selecting a suitable blank. I have chosen a teak blank because it has some attractive figure and is not a difficult wood to turn. Any close-grained wood that is not too hard would be suitable; fruitwoods such as apple and cherry are particularly good for beginners.

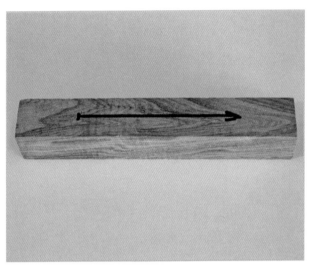

Step 2 Draw a line along the length of the wood with a marker pen and mark with an arrow the end that will be the nib end. This will ensure that once the blank is cut you can realign the components to keep the figure of the wood running through the finished pen. Misaligned figure can spoil the appearance of an otherwise well-made pen.

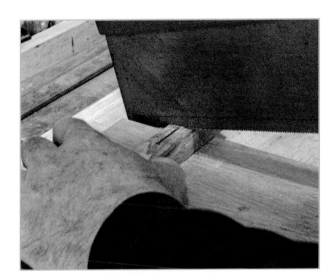

Step 3 Using one of the brass tubes from the kit as a guide, mark the blank about ⅛ in. (3mm) longer than the tube and cut to length. Here I am cutting by hand using a bench hook and tenon saw. Try to keep the cut reasonably square, but don't worry if it is a little off-line, this will be corrected when we trim the barrel in Step 8.

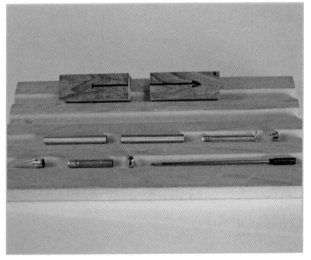

Step 4 Once the blank is cut to length I like to lay out all of the parts in order. This helps to ensure nothing is missing and can be very helpful in avoiding confusion with more complex kits, so it is a good habit to get into. A board with V-shaped grooves cut into it will help keep the components in place. Take care to lay the blank out the right way round. Here I have mistakenly laid the blank out with the end that will be at the nib end of the pen at the cap end.

Step 5 Now, using the 7-mm drill bit, drill carefully through the blank for the brass tube. The blank must be held firmly and square to the drill bit using one of the methods described in Chapter 2. Here I am using a power drill in a stand with a simple vise. Drill steadily and withdraw the bit frequently to keep the flutes clear. This will help ensure a straight bore and a clean exit hole with no breakout. Check that the brass tubes slide easily in and out of the blank without sticking.

Step 6 Lightly sand the brass tubes on a piece of 240-grit aluminum oxide abrasive to remove any contamination and to provide a good surface for the adhesive. Dirt or grease on the tubes can cause the glue joint to fail.

Step 7 Spread a little CA adhesive onto a tube, and spread it evenly onto the tube and the bore of the blank by inserting once from each end and twisting slightly. Then push the tube fully into the blank so that each end of the tube is about 1/16 in. (1.5mm) in from the end of the blank.

Step 8 Once the glue has dried, using one of the methods described in Chapter 2, square the end of the blanks with the tubes. Here I am using a barrel trimmer fitted into the body of an adjustable mandrel and I am turning the lathe spindle by hand. If you do this with the lathe running, use a clamp or similar device to hold the blank to avoid possible injury. Be careful not to turn away any of the brass tube as this may affect the fit of the mechanism later.

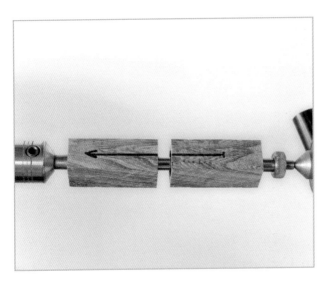

Step 9 Now the prepared barrels can be mounted on the mandrel, separated by one of the bushings and with another bushing at each end. Note how the components are aligned using the marking from Step 2 to keep the figure aligned and the pieces in the right order. All of the turning, sanding, and polishing will be done with the lathe speed set at about 2,500 rpm, so check the settings before you move on to Step 10.

Step 10 Begin to turn the blanks down to size using the spindle gouge. Remember to place the gouge firmly on the rest, rub the bevel, and then lift the handle until the edge begins to cut. Then move along the work. Taking light cuts, try to produce smooth, evenly shaped cylinders.

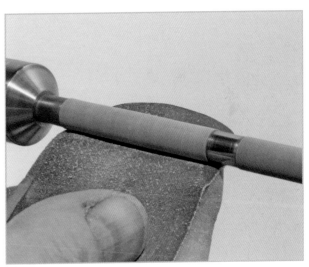

Step 11 Once the blanks are turned down most of the way to the bushings, use the skew chisel for the finishing cuts to bring them down almost to the bushings, leaving only a tiny margin for sanding. See how the chisel is aligned so that the cut is on the bottom third of the edge. Again, rub the bevel, lift until cutting begins, and then move along the work. Take care to avoid cutting with the top half of the skew and do not let either of the points come into contact with the work.

Step 12 Starting with 240-grit (320 if your skew work is very good), sand through the grits of aluminum oxide abrasive to 400. Between grits, dust off the work and apply a thin coat of cellulose sanding sealer. Continue sanding until the barrels are smooth and align perfectly with the bushings. Take care not to overdo it and sand the bushings, as you will wear them down and future pens will not be a good fit.

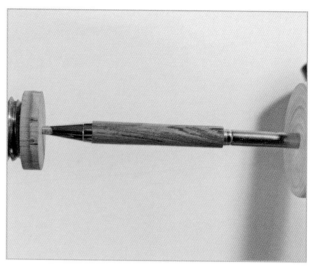

Step 13 Once you are happy that the barrels are smooth and aligned to the bushings, you can apply a finish. Any of the options described in Chapter 2 can be used but for this project I have used friction polish as it is one of the easiest to apply. Cover the barrels with a thin coat of the polish, turn on the lathe, and buff to a shine using the cloth that you used to apply the polish. The heat generated will bring the barrels to a high gloss. You can optionally apply a coat of microcrystalline wax to protect the finish.

Step 14 Now the components can be removed from the mandrel and they are ready to be assembled. With wooden inserts fitted to the head and tailstocks of the lathe I wind in the tailstock quill to press the parts into place. Begin by pressing in the nib unit and then the twist mechanism, which should be inserted up to the line marked on its barrel so that the refill protrudes by just the right amount when in use. Once the body is completed, the end cap can be passed through the clip and pressed into the other barrel. Take care to keep the parts aligned correctly for the figure of the wood.

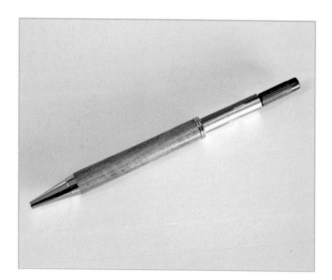

Step 15 The center band can now be slid over the mechanism and the refill screwed into place. All that remains is to press on the upper barrel, taking care to align the figure, and your Slimline pen is completed.

Technical **tip**

In order to ensure that the wooden barrels remain attached to the brass tubes, it is important to create sound glue joints. Whatever adhesive you choose, you should first of all check that you have a good sliding fit between the tube and the bore of the blank. Abrade the brass tube with fine abrasive paper to remove any contaminants and provide a key, and make sure that glue is spread evenly all over the joint by twisting the tube as it is inserted into the barrel. Finally, make sure the adhesive is fully set before doing any further work.

Variations

From top to bottom:

Gold Slimline "Greek Key" Pencil in Polar Ice acrylic

Gold Slimline Pen in pohutukawa

Gold Slimline Click Pencil in pohutukawa

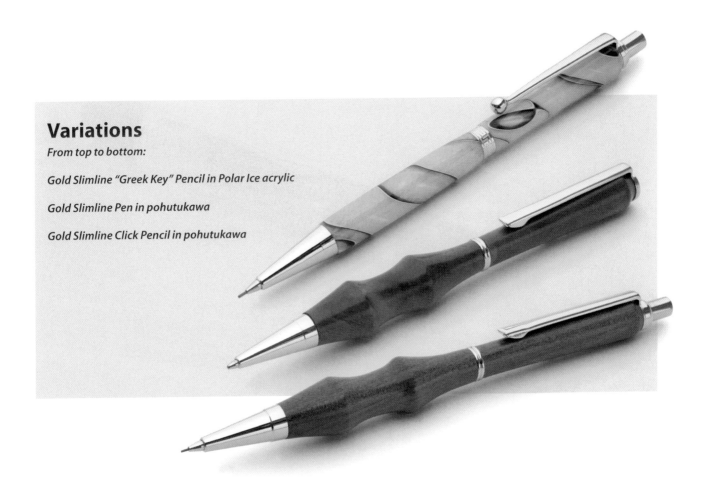

Acrylic Sierra Pen

The Sierra is a widely available and popular kit that lends itself to many different interpretations. Having a single barrel and a mechanism that assembles very easily, it is a good pen for the beginner, and yet it is versatile enough for the more advanced turner who wishes to experiment with more advanced techniques. This project is a relatively simple but attractive pen using an acrylic blank in red, gold, and green.

Tools and materials

Type-A mandrel and bushings for kit
$^{27}/_{64}$-in. drill bit
Acrylic blank 2½ in. (65mm) long
Barrel trimmer
Roughing gouge and skew chisel (or Spindlemaster)
CA or epoxy adhesive
240- and 320-grit aluminum oxide abrasive
Micromesh abrasives

Step 1 After cutting the blank about ¼in. (6mm) longer than the brass tube, the first task is to drill out the bore for the tube using a ²⁷⁄₆₄ in. drill bit. Here I am using a dedicated pen blank chuck and a bullet-point drill bit.

Step 2 Finish drilling just short of breaking through the blank and then trim the end back on the bandsaw, leaving a clean exit hole as shown here. You should leave the blank about ⅛ in. (3mm) longer than the tube to allow for squaring the ends.

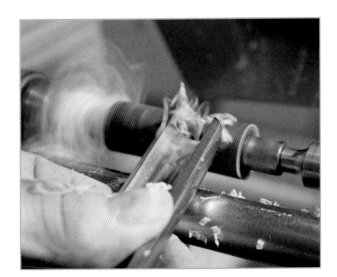

Step 3 Glue the tube into the blank with CA or epoxy and, when set, square the ends as described in Chapter 2. Mount the prepared blank on a mandrel using the appropriate bushings; I have used a collet chuck style mandrel for this project. Now begin to turn the blank to a cylinder using a roughing gouge. Remember to use sharp tools and take light cuts. Lathe speed should be about 2,500 rpm.

Step 4 Once the blank is turned down to approximate size you can begin to shape it using a skew chisel. If you find this tool difficult to use, the Spindlemaster is a suitable alternative. Try to produce a shape that blends in to match the shape of the other components and flows neatly to match the size of the bushings. A straight-sided barrel or one that has a slight curve will work equally well with the Sierra. Tidy up any irregularities using the shear-scraping technique described in Chapter 2.

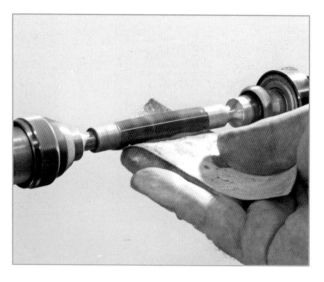

Step 5 Once the desired shape has been achieved, any remaining irregularities can be removed with abrasive cloth or paper, starting at about 240 or 320-grit before wet sanding with micromesh through all the grits from 1,500 to 12,000. Your blank should now look polished and should show no visible scratches.

Step 6 The final step before assembly is to buff the finished barrel on a cloth wheel using very fine polishing paste or plastic polish. Be careful to hold the component against the buffing wheel in the "safe" areas described in Chapter 2.

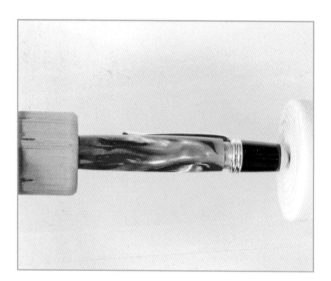

Step 7 The only mechanical assembly required for this kit is to press the top and clip, which come already assembled, into the top of the barrel. Any of the methods described in Chapter 2 can be used for this. Here we see the lathe being used as a press with wooden inserts in the head and tailstocks.

Step 8 The working end of the pen is assembled by simply inserting the refill and spring into the nib unit and screwing on the mechanism. Twist to check that it is working properly. It is as simple as changing the refill in a store-bought pen.

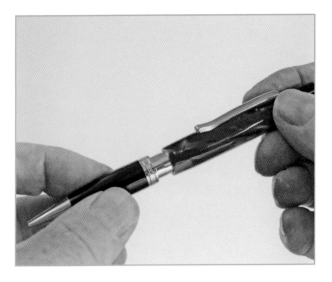

Technical **tip**

Some acrylic materials, especially the lighter colored ones, can be translucent and the brass tubes can show through the thinner parts. To avoid this, paint the tubes with a light-colored paint. You can either spray them with the cellulose or acrylic paint used for car bodies or brush on artists' acrylics. White or a matching color is best, and with very translucent tubes, painting the inside of the drilled tube can help, too.

Step 9 Finally, push the assembled mechanism into the completed barrel and your project is complete.

Variations

From top to bottom:

Acrylic Gold Polaris Pen

Acrylic Ultra Cigar Pen

Acrylic Classic Twist Pencil

BURL ELM FOUNTAIN PEN

Good quality fountain pen mechanisms deserve the finest barrels to enhance them, and by using burls it is possible to create very attractive pens. Exotic burls are highly prized and can be expensive, but native species can be just as attractive and offcuts of burl can often be obtained cheaply from furniture makers or from other turners. This pen is made from a blank cut from an elm burl given to me by a turner who makes much larger pieces and for whom these pieces were considered scrap.

Tools and materials

Junior Gentleman's (Gentleman's Classic) Fountain Pen kit
Mandrel and bushings for kit
10.5-mm and 12.5-mm drill bits
Two-part epoxy adhesive
Medium CA adhesive
Barrel trimmer
Roughing gouge and skew chisel (or Spindlemaster)
240- and 320-grit aluminum oxide abrasive
Micromesh abrasives

Step 1 If you have obtained an offcut of burl you will need to first of all cut it into suitably sized pen blanks. All of these blanks, which are ¾ in. (20mm) square were cut from a single small offcut of elm burl. Select a blank that is a suitable size using the brass tubes as a guide.

Step 2 Mark up the blank with a felt tip pen so that you can identify the grain orientation during drilling and preparation. Examine the figure of the blank carefully and decide which will be the barrel end and which the cap, and mark these accordingly. I use an arrow to identify the barrel end, and when assembling the pen I ensure that the figure matches when the cap is fitted. The blanks can now be cut to size, a little longer than the barrels to allow for trimming. I use my blank-cutting jig with the bandsaw.

Step 3 Drill the blanks starting from the inner end of each blank to ensure the best grain match. I used bullet point drills (10.5mm and 12.5mm) in a keyless chuck in the tailstock while the blanks were held in a chuck fitted with pin jaws.

Step 4 It is important that the holes drilled through the barrels are a good fit and are concentric. Poorly fitting tubes can result in misshapen barrels and a poor fit with the components. The brass tubes should slide easily into the holes without sticking and without any sloppiness or gaps. Test the fit before gluing the tubes in place with two-part epoxy adhesive. You can use CA glue for this but for better quality pens I prefer epoxy.

Step 5 Once the glue is set (I always leave epoxy overnight to harden, even the quick-setting types), the tubes can be trimmed square. Here I have used a shopmade jig with a sanding disk in the lathe. You can use any of the methods described in Chapter 2.

Step 6 The prepared blanks are now ready to be mounted on the lathe. Remember to keep the parts correctly oriented for grain match. Here the blanks are mounted on an adjustable double mandrel and held in place using a mandrel saver.

Step 7 Turn the blanks down almost to size using a spindle roughing gouge and skew chisel (or Spindlemaster) as described in Chapter 2. Do not turn right down to the bushings yet to allow for further trimming in the next step.

Step 8 Burls often contain small voids and defects that need filling. Where these are shallow, fill them with thick CA but if they go right through to the brass tubes then a mixture of CA and sawdust is needed to prevent the tubes showing through the finished barrel. Once set (you can use an accelerator spray), turn down the barrels almost to the bushings, sand to final size and fit with aluminum oxide abrasive. Make a final check for defects, repeating the process of filling and sanding as necessary.

Step 9 The pen is finished with medium CA, using the technique outlined in Chapter 2. Two or three coats of CA should be applied, followed by sanding through the grits of micromesh and polishing on the buffing wheel with white diamond compound.

Step 10 Finally assemble the pen by pressing the components into the barrels as shown in the instructions supplied by the manufacturers. Here I am using a bench vise protected by MDF jaws to press the components together. The completed pen can be given a protective coat of microcrystalline wax to protect the finish and prevent fingerprints.

Technical **tip**

Burls and spalted wood can be fragile to turn. It helps to stabilize them with CA glue before and during turning. My method is to give the blank a coat of thin CA, allowing it to soak into the wood and then, once it is turned down almost to the bushings, apply a coat of thin or medium CA between each grit.

Variations

From top to bottom:

Gold Sierra Twist Pen in burl elm

Gold Classic Fountain pen in myrtle burl

Rhodium Gentleman's Classic Fountain pen in Honduran rosewood burl

EL DIABLO PANACHE PEN

The Panache pen kit, which is available in gold, black, chrome, or rhodium plating, is a modern design that has no clip but is designed to stand on end on a desk or table. This is a large pen and requires a blank 1 in. (25mm) in cross section. The El Diablo blank is an attractive red and black swirl acrylic.

Tools and materials

El Diablo or similar blank at least 1 in. (25mm)
    in diameter and 6 in. (150mm) long
Type-A mandrel and bushings for kit
13/32-in. and 12.5-mm drill bits
Roughing gouge and skew chisel (or Spindlemaster)
CA or epoxy adhesive
240-, 320-, and 400-grit aluminum oxide abrasive
Micromesh abrasives

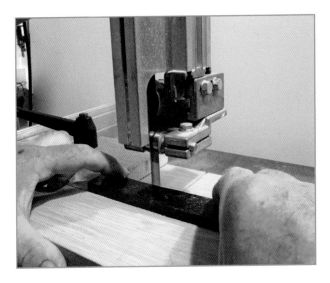

Step 1 Begin by cutting the blank to length. With the El Diablo blank, which is only 5¼ in. (133mm) long there is not much to spare. Care is needed to measure accurately and there is no scope for my tip of cutting the blank long and drilling short to avoid breakout. Here I am cutting the blank to length using my cutting jig on the bandsaw.

Step 2 Drill the blanks carefully and slowly to avoid breakout. Drilling at slow speed on the lathe using bullet point bits will produce the best results with the least risk of breakout. Withdraw the bit regularly to clear the shavings and avoid overheating. Take care to drill the larger ½-in. (12.5-mm) hole through the longer part of the blank, which will form the cap end of the finished pen.

Step 3 Glue in the tubes in the usual way using CA or epoxy and leave to set. When the glue is fully cured, use a blank trimmer or disk sander and jig to square off the ends of the blanks. The example here has been trimmed back using a disk sander until just flush with the end of the brass tube.

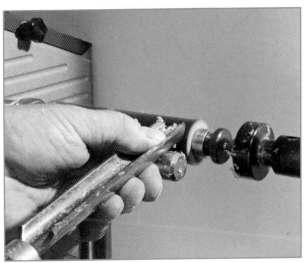

Step 4 Because of the stylish curved shape of the Panache, there is a lot of acrylic to remove in the middle section, so begin by using a roughing gouge to establish the basic shape. Do not be over zealous. Turning acrylic requires sharp tools and light cuts. If you take too heavy a cut you will cause chipping.

Step 5 As the acrylic blank moves from square to cylindrical, the shavings will start to come off in long thin strands. These will tend to wrap themselves around the work and the mandrel, preventing you from seeing what you are doing. Remove them regularly to avoid a buildup. With the lathe running I prefer to use a stiff brush, which is not only more effective than using your fingers but is safer, too.

Step 6 It helps to turn with a plain background behind the lathe so that you can stand back and check that the profile is developing properly and that there are no extraneous lumps and bumps.

Step 7 Here I am using a skew chisel as a scraper to finalize the shape of the blank. A Spindlemaster or other negative rake scraper is a suitable alternative.

Step 8 Once you have achieved the desired shape, sand the blank through the grits to 400. Once sanded, finally check over the shape to ensure that you have a nice flowing form and then wet sand with micromesh to a finish. When wet sanding I cover the lathe bed with a microfiber cloth or thick paper towels to protect it from the water. Keep the micromesh wet and wipe the blank to remove slurry between each grit.

Step 9 Finally, buff to a high gloss with white diamond compound on a buffing wheel before assembling the kit in accordance with the manufacturer's instructions. Here I am using wooden inserts in the head and tailstock and pressing the components together by winding in the tailstock quill.

Technical **tip**

Wet sanding with micromesh is a great way of getting a fine finish on your acrylic projects but do take care when using this method, bearing in mind that water and machinery do not go well together. Not only will water splashed onto the lathe bed cause corrosion, but water must also be kept well away from the motor and other electrical components. This is especially important where the motor is under the lathe bed, as it is in some smaller lathes. Protect the lathe using old cloths or towels and make sure that any splashes are dried off immediately.

Variations

From top to bottom:

Chrome Panache Pen in cocobolo

Black Chrome Panache Pen in Midnight Reef acrylic

Rhodium Panache Pen in amboyna burl

Tigerwood Classic Twist Pen

Pen blanks made from laminated colored veneers make attractive pieces and are available under a number of trade names, such as Tigerwood, ColorWood, and Colorply®. For this project I have used a Tigerwood blank along with a Classic Twist Pen kit. This is the type of kit that many beginners to pen making move on to once they have mastered the Slimline or Streamline kits.

Tools and materials

Laminated veneer Tigerwood pen blank
Classic Twist Pen kit
Type-B (8-mm) mandrel and bushings for kit
8.2-mm drill bit
Two-part epoxy adhesive
Medium CA adhesive
Barrel trimmer
Roughing gouge and skew chisel (or Spindlemaster)
240- and 320-grit aluminum oxide abrasive
Micromesh abrasives

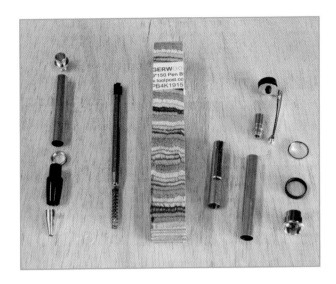

Step 1 Lay out all the components in order to check that your kit is complete and to understand how the components will be assembled. Refer to the manufacturer's instructions if necessary. Here the components are laid out in order along with the blank.

Step 2 Use the brass tubes supplied with the kit to set up your saw so that the blank is cut about ⅛in. (3mm) longer than the tube to allow for trimming. Here I am using a shopmade jig with the bandsaw, but a tablesaw, scrollsaw, or miter saw would be just as effective. The important thing is to make an accurate cut to the correct length—too short and the brass tube will protrude from the blank, too long and trimming will become a chore.

Step 3 Before cutting the two blanks, the original blank is marked up to ensure that the pattern of the veneers is aligned in the finished pen. This is particularly important with laminated pens as any misalignment will be very obvious in the finished pen.

Step 4 Drill the blanks starting from the inner end of each blank. Drilling from the middle to the ends will also help to ensure the best veneer pattern alignment. Here I am using a bullet-point drill bit in a power drill mounted in a stand. The blank is held steady in a dedicated pen blank drilling vise that ensures it is held vertical. The scrap piece in the base of the vise helps to prevent breakout when the drill emerges from the end of the blank.

Step 5 With the brass tubes inserted, the ends of the barrels are now trimmed square and flush with the ends of the tubes. For this project I used a barrel trimmer fitted in a cordless drill while the blank was held firmly in the bench vise. Take care not to overtighten the vise as excessive pressure could split the blank or deform the brass tube.

Step 6 This kit requires the use of a type-B mandrel, which is larger in diameter than the standard type-A mandrel. Here the blanks are mounted on the lathe in a double mandrel and I have fitted a longer tool rest to the lathe so I can work on both ends of the pen without having to move the rest.

Step 7 Turn the blanks down to size as described in Chapter 2 using a roughing gouge and skew chisel. Leave the finished blanks just a little proud of the bushings. (Here I have left a little more than usual to compensate for wear in the bushings, which are due for replacement.) Mark a point exactly 3/16 in. (5mm) from the inner end of the thicker (cap) blank and then, turning the lathe by hand, extend the mark into a line all the way around the blank.

Step 8 With a very sharp parting tool, cut back from the end of the barrel to the line you have just marked, removing the wood all the way back to the brass tube. Cutting this recess enables the center band to be fitted and accuracy is required to ensure a good fit. Some kits require a tenon to be cut that does not go all the way down to the tube. Check with the instructions supplied with your kit and if this is the case turn carefully to the specified dimensions.

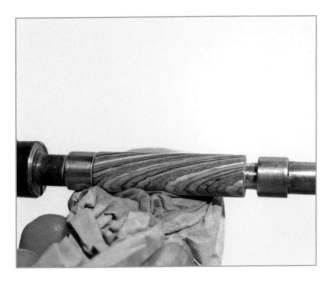

Step 9 Colored veneer laminate blanks are impregnated with resin and can be finished by sanding and polishing with abrasives without the need for an applied finish. If you wish, you can apply a finish of your choice, but for this project the pen was sanded through the grits of aluminum oxide abrasive followed by micromesh and buffing with white diamond compound. This produces a satin or semigloss finish. A high gloss could be achieved by using CA or friction polish.

Step 10 The finished components can now be assembled, taking care to include the various rings and bands in the appropriate places as per the instructions or drawing provided with your kit. Here I am using a bench vise, protected with MDF jaws, to press the parts together. The brass threads of the center connector are protected using a short piece of tube or a spare bushing, as pressing directly on the end of this delicate brass component is likely to cause damage. When assembling, take care to align the pattern of the veneers. Here I have aligned the pattern so that the two halves mirror each other when the point is withdrawn and it is continuous when the pen is twisted and the refill is extended.

Technical **tip**

With some types of laminated materials the color from the darker colored bands can contaminate the lighter colored ones during sanding. To avoid this I apply a thin coat of sanding sealer or CA before beginning sanding and again between each grit of abrasive. This prevents particles from the darker colored bands finding their way into the pores of the wood and causing staining.

Variations

From top to bottom:

Gold Classic Pencil in blue/yellow Tigerwood

Gold Classic Ballpoint Pen in multicolored Tigerwood

Gold Classic Fountain Pen in red/grey Tigerwood

ENGLISH YEW
JUNIOR GENTLEMAN'S PENCIL

This pencil is made from a blank of English yew. It is not highly figured, as a burl would be, and nor is it an exotic or expensive wood. Nonetheless, it demonstrates that the beautiful color and grain of wood that can be obtained cheaply and locally is often enough to show off the classic proportions and attractive plating of a quality writing instrument. In this case the kit is a Junior Gentleman's Pencil in 10k gold.

Tools and materials

Yew pen blank ¾ in. (20mm) x ¾ in. (20mm)
Junior Gentleman's Pencil kit
Mandrel and bushings for kit
25⁄64-in. and 15⁄32-in. drill bits
Two-part epoxy adhesive
Medium CA adhesive
Barrel trimmer
Roughing gouge and skew chisel (or Spindlemaster)
240-, 320- and 400-grit aluminum oxide abrasive
Micromesh abrasives

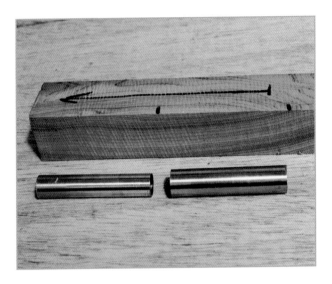

Step 1 After checking that your kit is complete and laying out the components to understand how the pencil will be assembled, mark up the blank using the brass tubes to set the length of each barrel, making a small ⅛-in. (3-mm) allowance for trimming square and marking the blank with an arrow to indicate the nib end of the kit.

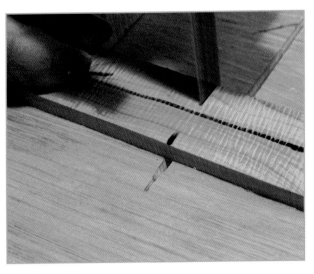

Step 2 Using a bandsaw or whatever is your preferred choice of saw, cut the blanks accurately to the measured length. If using a powered saw, do take care to keep your fingers well clear of the blade by using a push stick, jig, or clamp as appropriate for the machine. Powered miter saws, for example, will lift small pieces such as pen blanks from the bed of the machine so the workpiece must be securely clamped.

Step 3 Drill the blanks, working out from the center toward the ends as indicated by your marking out. Here I am using a power drill in a stand, with the blank securely held in a machine vise. Clamping is vital to ensure accuracy and safety. The cap end of the pencil is drilled to $\frac{25}{64}$ in. and the longer nib end is drilled to $\frac{15}{32}$ in.

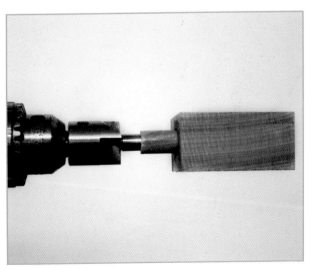

Step 4 Trim the ends of the blanks square using a barrel trimmer or disk sander. When using a barrel trimmer you should ensure that the shaft of the trimmer is a good fit in the tube by fitting a shaft or sleeve of the appropriate size. Here the blank that takes the wider of the tubes is prepared for trimming using a shopmade hardwood sleeve.

Step 5 Mount the blanks on your mandrel using the bushings for the kit, taking care to align them using your marked arrow to ensure the correct orientation of the figure. Turn each blank down to a cylinder using the spindle roughing gouge and then down almost to the bushings with the skew, ensuring a smooth, flowing curve from center to tip. Leave only enough to allow for final sanding.

Step 6 Once the barrels are shaped to your satisfaction you are ready to begin finishing by sanding through the grits of aluminum oxide paper, starting with the finest grit that will remove any marks left from the tools and ending with 400-grit.

Step 7 Wipe the blank with methyl hydrate or cellulose thinners to remove any residues and then apply a CA finish using the procedure outlined in Chapter 2. Sanding with 1,500-grit micromesh between each coat will ensure any lines or ridges are removed. Three or more coats will be needed to achieve a good quality finish.

Step 8 Once the finish has hardened, polish through the grits of micromesh from 1,500 to 12,000. It may not be necessary to use all the grits. Stepping from 1,500 to 2,400, then to 4,000, and then to 12,000 will work just fine. The barrels can now be removed from the mandrel.

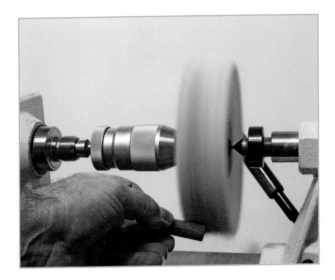

Step 9 The final polish is achieved by buffing the completed barrels on a cloth wheel using white diamond compound. An alternative is to use plastic polish, the kind used for polishing scratches out of motorcycle helmets, applied with a cloth while the blanks are still on the lathe.

Step 10 The finished components can now be assembled in accordance with the instructions or drawing provided with your kit. Here I am using a bench vise to press the parts together. The pencil mechanism of this kit comes assembled to the other components and will need to be taken apart before assembly by unscrewing the black twist mechanism from the plated center coupling and withdrawing the pencil mechanism. Once the center coupling and tip have been pressed into place, the mechanism may be reassembled by reversing the above procedure.

Technical **tip**

When applying a CA finish, the bushings can tend to get stuck to the finished barrel. To avoid this problem many people wax the ends of the bushings, but a better alternative is to remount the barrels between centers or between cone bushings before beginning the finishing process. Using this method the CA adhesive never comes into contact with the bushings or centers and the problem simply does not arise.

Variations

From top to bottom:

Gold Junior Gentleman's Pencil in swamp totara

Gold Regency style Pencil in English yew

Black Titanium Sierra Pencil in English yew

ARTIST'S SKETCH PENCIL

Several types of artist's sketch pencil, with a thick, soft lead, are available, but for this project I chose the dns-Pencil kit because it uses some techniques not found in other projects. The kit doesn't require the use of a normal mandrel and bushings, although the special mandrel designed specifically for this kit, while not essential, will greatly facilitate ease of making. The pen blank is ziricote, a very dense wood often used in the making of guitars that requires sharp tools to turn it successfully.

Tools and materials

dns-Pencil kit
Special mandrel for kit (optional)
9mm and 7.5mm drill bits or stepped drill bit
Ziricote blank 6 in. (150mm) long
   by ½ in. (13mm) square
Barrel trimmer
Roughing gouge and skew chisel (or Spindlemaster)
Medium CA and epoxy adhesives
240- and 320-grit aluminum oxide abrasive
Micromesh abrasives

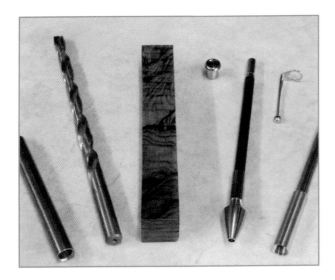

Step 1 Assemble the necessary components, wooden blank, and tools required. The kit appears deceptively simple, consisting of a single brass tube and preassembled mechanism, but take a look at the step in the tube and the fact that the wider end of the tube is threaded internally to accept the mechanism, and clearly the normal mandrel and bushings method is not going to be suitable. To the left of the photo are the special mandrel, which is threaded to fit the brass tube, and a stepped drill bit. These are optional but they do make the process much easier.

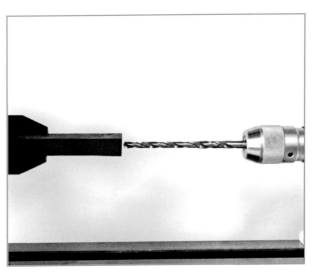

Step 2 Begin by cutting the blank a tiny bit longer than the brass tube and then drill the hole for the tube using a 9-mm drill followed by a long 7.5-mm drill or a suitable stepped drill. The 9-mm section of the hole needs to have a finished length of 1⁹⁄₁₆ in. (40mm) to accommodate the thicker part of the brass tube, so it should be drilled to this depth plus a small allowance for squaring the end with the barrel trimmer. As this is a long blank, careful setting up and accurate drilling are essential.

Step 3 Once the blank has been drilled, check the fit of the barrel. Using the special mandrel helps with insertion and removal. When happy with the fit, glue the tube into the prepared blank and leave it to set. The manufacturers suggest using their own adhesive, a polyurethane glue, but I find that epoxy also works well. Once again, the special mandrel helps with insertion and also helps keep the screw threads free from adhesive, but remember to remove it before leaving to set.

Step 4 The instructions are specific about the finished length of the barrel at 113.8mm or 113.3mm if the clip is to be used. I find that there is leeway within the fit of the mechanism to cope with minor variations and, as long as the ends of the blank are trimmed exactly to the ends of the brass tube, everything will fit. Here I am using my shop-made holding device while trimming the blank with the barrel trimmer fitted in the headstock. Take care not to damage the screw threads in the brass tube.

Step 5 Once set, the prepared blank can be mounted on the lathe. Here I have used the special mandrel mounted in a keyless chuck in the headstock, but you could turn a suitable spigot about 1¼ in. (30mm) long and exactly 9mm in diameter from scrap hardwood and mount the tube on this. The other end of the blank is supported by a revolving center in the tailstock. (Take care not to over tighten the tailstock as this can damage or flare the end of the brass tube).

Step 6 Use a spindle roughing gouge to turn the blank down to a cylinder just a little larger in diameter than the required finished size. About ⅝ in. (16mm) should be fine. If you have used ziricote or a similarly hard wood as your blank, you will need to make sure your gouge is very sharp and you may need to hone it several times as work progresses to ensure a clean cut.

Step 7 Now turn to the skew chisel to bring the diameter of the "nib" end of the pencil down to a little above the final finished diameter. An exact fit to the 13-mm nib unit is required, so check regularly using digital calipers. Here the diameter is down to 13.3mm and final sanding will remove the final three tenths of a millimeter for a good fit.

Step 8 Continue shaping with the skew chisel to reduce the other end of the barrel to fit the clip and end cap (11mm) and to form an attractive overall shape. Here at 11.8mm there is still a little way to go. With careful cuts, the tearout from the roughing gouge that can be seen on the barrel will also be removed. Once the skew chisel work is completed and you have sanded through the grits of aluminum oxide abrasive up to 400-grit, the blank should be ready for final finishing.

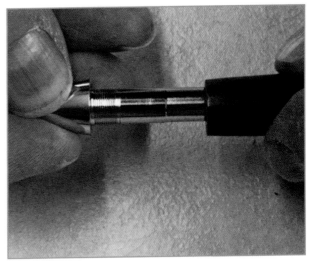

Step 9 The pen is finished with medium CA, using the technique outlined in Chapter 2. Two or three coats of CA should be applied, followed by sanding through the grits of micromesh and polishing on the buffing wheel with white diamond compound. Here I am using 1,500-grit micromesh to smooth down the CA between coats.

Step 10 Assemble the pencil by pressing the top and clip unit into the top end of the barrel. Take care to align the recess on the underside of the end cap with the pressed dimple on the clip. This will ensure a good fit and prevent the clip from turning. The preassembled mechanism can now be screwed into the barrel to complete the pencil.

Technical **tip**
Pens and pencils with long single barrels like this are an excellent medium for showing off finely figured wood and burls, but when combined with some of the other techniques described in this book they can make something really special. A barrel decorated with inlays, such as in the Celtic Knot project, or patterned using texturing or a Pen Wizard would work particularly well.

Variations
From top to bottom:

Chrome Artist's Sketch Pencil in bog oak

Chrome Artist's Sketch Pencil in reclaimed mahogany

Chrome Artist's Sketch Pencil in multicolor acrylic

POLYMER CLAY PEN

It is possible to buy ready-made polymer clay blanks, but this pen is for those who want to make their own blanks. The project is based upon a technique for making blanks without turning the tubes, but has been modified to suit those who prefer to turn the blanks to fit. If you prefer to use the manual methods you can follow the steps up to Step 8 and then finish the tube by hand-sanding and buffing.

Tools and materials

A suitable pen kit such as the Sierra
Polymer clay for a base layer
Pasta machine or roller
Premade millefiori canes (unless you make your own)
A sharp blade
Stove
Mandrel and bushings appropriate to the kit you are using
Skew chisel (or Spindlemaster)
Micromesh abrasives
Medium CA glue (optional)
Buffing wheel and white diamond compound

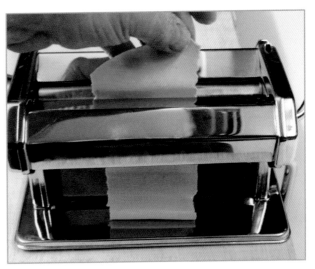

Step 1 A sheet of polymer clay (PC) is used to cover the brass pen tube, but PC needs to be conditioned before you use it. To condition the clay you can roll it on a tile to make it soft and pliable or you can run it through a pasta machine until you don't see any cracks.

Step 2 Once the clay is conditioned, run it through the pasta machine to create a thin sheet. Keep your machine only for use with polymer clay and do not subsequently use it for pasta. A good secondhand machine is a better buy than a cheap new one.

Step 3 Wrap this sheet of clay around the tube, cutting at the join with a very sharp blade.

Step 4 Check that the clay is adhering evenly to the tube and smooth out the seam.

Step 5 Take a prepared millefiori cane and cut slices off using a sharp blade, slicing them as thin as possible if finishing by hand or a little thicker if you plan to turn the blank to shape.

Step 6 Apply these slices onto the tube. The PC sheet that is wrapped around it acts like glue, so once you have positioned a slice on the tube do not try to move it or the clay will rip. Think carefully about how you want the design to look and plan the positioning of the pieces before you start putting them on.

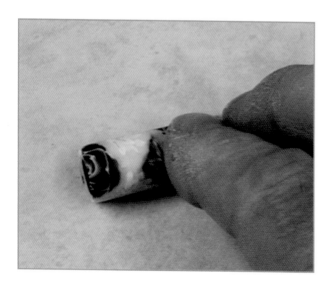

Step 7 After you have applied a few slices, roll the work on a large plain ceramic tile. A marble or granite surface or a piece of float glass is a suitable alternative, but the surface must not be textured! Apply only light pressure when rolling. Then apply more slices and roll again. Continue to add slices and roll until you have covered the tube.

Step 8 While you are rolling the tube, clay will begin to move to the ends. Use your blade to slice off the clay that is not adhering to the tube.

Step 9 When you have completed the rolling and the blank is smooth, place the tube on a flat tile standing upright. Bake it in the oven according to the manufacturer's directions, usually for 30 to 40 minutes. Here is the finished piece ready to be positioned for baking.

Step 10 Once it has cooled, you have a blank ready for turning on the lathe (or, if you prefer, you can jump to Step 13 and start sanding by hand). Mount the blank on the lathe using the bushings and mandrel.

Step 11 Turn the blank to the required size using a sharp skew chisel and light cuts. Take care not to cut too deeply, as you will turn away the millefiori you have just carefully positioned.

Step 12 Sand the blank with the lathe running at about 500 rpm, working through the grades of micromesh until you have a good finish.

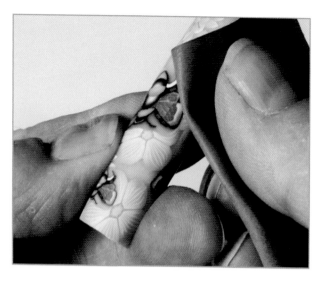

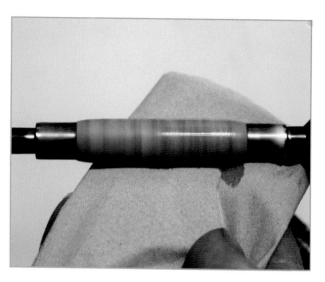

Step 13 If you are finishing the blank by hand, begin sanding with 600- or 800-grit abrasive, again being careful not to sand right through the millefiori. Sand until you have it nice and smooth, and then move onto the next grit, continuing through the grits to 12,000.

Step 14 If you wish, at this stage you can apply a CA finish to the blank as described in Chapter 2.

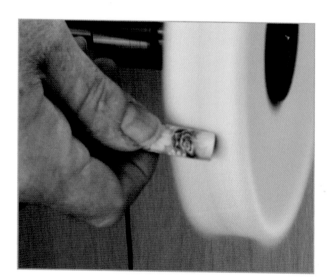

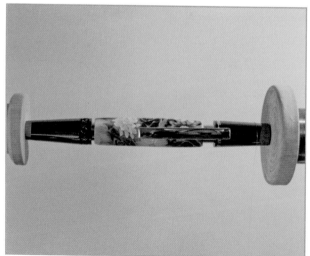

Step 15 Buff the finished piece on a buffing wheel to a glasslike finish and then, if you have not applied a CA finish, apply a suitable polish, such as microcrystalline wax, to seal it.

Step 16 Assemble your pen in accordance with the manufacturer's instructions.

Technical **tip**

Polymer clay needs to be kneaded to make it pliable before beginning work. If this is not done thoroughly it will crack or crumble when baked or during turning or finishing. You can use the pasta machine to do this or you can simply work it by hand by rolling and folding it on a tile or other smooth surface.

Variations

From top to bottom:

Rhodium Elegant Beauty Pen with mixed polymer clay millefiori

Chrome Sierra Pen with kaleidoscopic polymer clay blank by Toni Ransfield

Rhodium Junior Gentleman's Rollerball Pen with blue polymer clay millefiori flowers and bees

MODIFIED SLIMLINE PEN

Most pen makers eventually like to move away from the constraints of standard kits and start experimenting with their own designs. This can lead to the development of more advanced techniques and even to making pens from scratch, buying in only components such as nibs and pencil mechanisms. Such advanced techniques are beyond the scope of this book, but for those who wish to make a start on kit modification, this fairly simple adaptation of the Slimline kit may give you some ideas.

Tools and materials

Slimline Pen kit
Mandrel and bushings for kit
7-mm drill bit
Contrasting pen blanks with a combined size of at least
6 in. (150mm) long by ⅝ in. (16mm) square
Barrel trimmer
Roughing gouge and skew chisel (or Spindlemaster)
CA and epoxy adhesive
240- and 320-grit aluminum oxide abrasive
Micromesh abrasives

Step 1 For this project you will need two pen blanks in contrasting species. I have used offcuts of rosewood and eucalyptus. One of the blanks will end up shorter than the brass tubes, the other will end up a little longer, but the overall dimensions will be the same as a standard slimline, so the total length of the blanks will need to be a little over the total length of the tubes to allow for trimming.

Step 2 Drill out both blanks to fit the tubes using the 7-mm drill and any of the methods outlined in Chapter 2. I find drilling on the lathe using a dedicated pen blank chuck or a chuck with pin jaws to be the most accurate way of drilling longer blanks.

Step 3 Glue the tubes into the blanks using CA or epoxy adhesive. The tube should protrude from one end of the shorter blank, and in the longer blank the tube should be almost flush with the clip end, leaving the bottom part of the blank free to accept the brass tube that protrudes from the end of the shorter blank when the pen is assembled.

Step 4 Square off both ends of the longer blank and the end of the shorter blank which is flush with the end of the brass tube. The end with the protruding tube will be squared off in Step 6.

Step 5 Mount the longer barrel onto a mandrel in the normal way and turn it down to a cylinder so that all the wood outside the diameter of the squared part of the end is removed and so that the barrel will sit flush with the shorter barrel when mounted together in Step 7.

Step 6 Now mount the shorter barrel onto the mandrel and carefully square off the end of the blank where the tube is exposed using a parting tool or, as I have done here, the point of a skew chisel. Take care to get this absolutely square, as the two barrels fit flush up to one another without any metal components and need to be an exact fit or there will be a gap showing when the pen is completed.

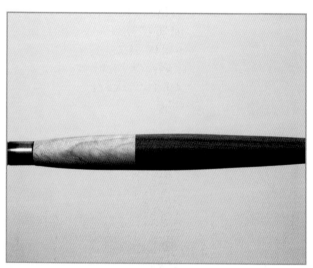

Step 7 The two halves of the pen can now be mounted together on the mandrel ready for turning to shape. Make sure that the fit is good where they join and if necessary go back to the previous steps and correct any inaccuracies.

Step 8 Using a spindle roughing gouge and skew chisel, turn the combined blank to an attractive shape, turning the ends down to the bushings in the normal way to fit the nib and clip fittings. As there is no center band there is nothing to constrain the shape of the pen, so you have free rein to use your creative skills. I have created a simple cigar shape but you may want to include ergonomic finger grips or other shaping.

Step 9 The pen can now be sanded and finished using any of the methods described in Chapter 2, but it is best to sand and finish each half of the pen separately to avoid staining of the grain by contrasting sawdust from the other half. Take care when sanding not to spoil the fit where the two parts join. Here the shorter barrel is being finished with CA.

Step 10 The pen is assembled by pressing together the components in the usual manner. Here you can see what the nib end should look like, with the brass tube and mechanism protruding from shorter part of the barrel. The cap and clip are pressed into the end of the longer barrel, which then slides over the bottom barrel with its brass tube engaging with the mechanism.

Technical **tip**

The design element of pen and pencil projects is just as important as the making. If you plan to make something that deviates from the original design of the pen or pencil, it is always a good idea to sit down with a pencil and paper or CAD software on your computer and draw out your design first. It is much easier to refine the design in this way than it is when the blanks are on the lathe.

Variations
From top to bottom:

*Modified Gold Slimline Pen
in rosewood and euclayptus*

*Modified Gold Slimline Pen
in euclayptus with rosewood center band*

Modified Gold Slimline Pen in cocobolo and rimu

CELTIC KNOT PEN

Interesting patterns and inlays can be incorporated into the design of pens and pencils by the insertion of veneers of contrasting wood or even of thin plastic or aluminum sheet. This project shows how to incorporate an attractive Celtic knot motif into a Sierra Vista pen. A strong contrast between the main wood of the pen and the inlay is important, and in this instance I chose rosewood and sycamore.

Tools and materials

Sierra Vista Pen kit
Mandrel and bushings for kit
$^{27}\!/_{64}$-in. drill bit
Rosewood blank at least 6 in. (150mm) long
   by $^{5}\!/_{8}$ in. (16mm) square
Sycamore or other light-colored veneer
Barrel trimmer
Roughing gouge and skew chisel (or Spindlemaster)
CA and epoxy adhesive
240- and 320-grit aluminum oxide abrasive
Micromesh abrasives

Step 1 For this project I cut and prepared my own veneer from a piece of sycamore. This is easy to do if you have a bandsaw, but do take care and use a push stick for safety. The cut veneer will need to be sanded to remove any saw marks. Cutting your own veneer makes it easy to match the veneer thickness to the thickness of your saw cut. Of course, it is possible to buy in suitable veneer if you do not have the facility to make your own.

Step 2 You can set up jigs on your bandsaw for this project but here I have used a hand miter saw of the type used by picture framers, as this already has the necessary depth stops built in and it is easy to create a length stop using a spare pen blank. The depth stops are set so that the cut is a little short of going all the way through the blank. The length is set so that the blank is fully supported by the bed of the saw and the cut is centered approximately where the pattern is to be. The pitch of the knot loops can be varied by altering the angle of the sawblade; here I have used a 45° angle.

Step 3 Check carefully that the veneer is a good fit in the saw cut. It should be a good sliding fit with no gaps but not so tight as to open up the cut and distort the blank. Sand the veneer by hand if necessary to reduce the thickness. Once a good fit has been achieved, use a sharp knife to cut off a suitable length of veneer.

Step 4 Glue the veneer in place using epoxy or thick CA adhesive. The edges of the veneer should be a little proud of the blank to allow for trimming. Leave the blank until the adhesive is fully cured before moving on to the next step. Do not be tempted to start the next cut before the blank is solid. This is not a process that can be rushed, and too much haste can ruin all your previous work.

Step 5 Once the veneer is firmly set in place, trim away the excess with a sharp knife or chisel. Do not worry if there is a little tearout at this stage, as it will be turned away as the barrel shape is formed, but the sharper the tool you use, the cleaner the cut will be.

Step 6 Now place the blank back on the saw, turned 90° from the previous cut as shown here. Make another cut as before and repeat Steps 3 to 5. Continue in this way until four veneer inserts have been glued in place, one from each side of the blank.

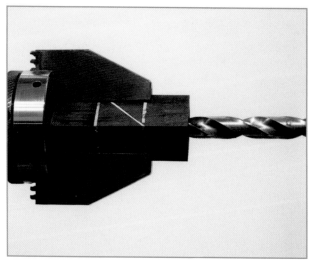

Step 7 Using the brass tube from the kit as a guide, mark off the length of the blank, positioning the inserts for the knot as required. Here I have centered them, but you may want the knot to be nearer the top or the nib end of your pen or pencil. Cut the blank to length using the bandsaw or whatever method you prefer.

Step 8 Carefully drill the blank to fit the brass tube. If your gluing was done well and the adhesive has been allowed to cure properly, a slow speed and careful drilling will ensure that the blank remains intact. Whatever drilling method you use, the blank must be well supported and care taken to ensure a good, straight bore is achieved.

Step 9 Using epoxy adhesive, glue the brass tube into the blank in the normal way as described in Chapter 2. I prefer epoxy adhesive rather than CA for this type of work as it creates a more reliable joint. Once the adhesive is set, trim the ends of the barrel with a barrel trimmer and then mount it on the lathe using the bushings and mandrel.

Step 10 Turn the barrel to shape using a spindle roughing gouge and skew chisel as described in Chapter 2. Make sure your tools are sharp and take very light cuts to avoid tearing out pieces of veneer or small pieces of the substrate blank. As you turn the barrel to shape, the outline of the Celtic knot pattern will begin to appear. Once the barrel is shaped, it can be sanded and finished using any of the methods described in this book. Do take care when sanding to avoid discoloration of the light veneer by the darker base wood. This can be avoided by sealing with sanding sealer or thin CA between each grit. I have used CA as finish for this pen.

Technical **tip**

To maintain an even appearance to the lines of the knot it is important to ensure that the veneers you use are of even thickness. If you use commercially produced veneers this will not be a problem, but when cutting your own veneers on the bandsaw take care to check the thickness and adjust using a hand-sanding block before beginning work on your project.

Variations
From top to bottom:

Gold, Titanium, and Chrome Majestic Squire Pen in sycamore with American black walnut Celtic knot pattern

Gunmetal Vertex Pen in sycamore with walnut inlaid pattern

Gold Streamline Pen in pearwood with walnut inlaid pattern

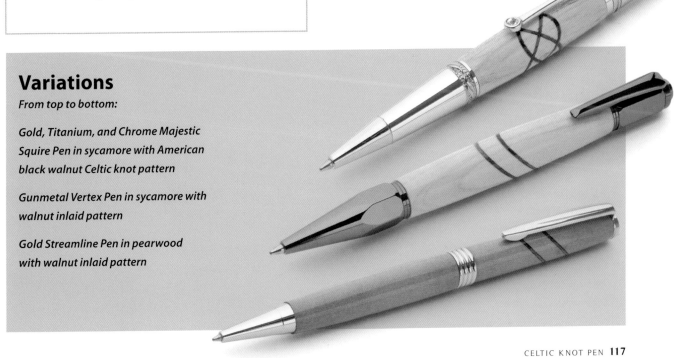

Segmented Sierra Pencil

Segmented work can create very attractive and unusual pieces and even beginner pen makers can create a simple checkerboard or harlequin-style design. The Sierra pencil is ideal for a first attempt at segmented work as the maker does not have to worry about aligning the segmentation across two barrels. For this project I have used cocobolo and boxwood, which have a strong and attractive contrast.

Tools and materials

Sierra Pencil kit
Mandrel and bushings for kit
$^{27}/_{64}$-in. drill bit
Cocobolo and boxwood blanks 6 in. (150mm)
    long by $^{1}/_{2}$ in. (13mm) square
Barrel trimmer
Roughing gouge and skew chisel (or Spindlemaster)
White woodworking adhesive
CA and epoxy adhesive
240- and 320-grit aluminum oxide abrasive
Micromesh abrasives

Step 1 Square up one face and one edge of each blank with a hand plane or on your planer. If using a planer, take care to use a push stick and follow all health and safety guidance. With woodworking adhesive, glue together the edges with the faces true to one another on a flat surface, clamp up, and leave overnight to set. Once set, cut in half across the width and glue the faces together, clamp up again, and leave to set. Here we see the completed blank.

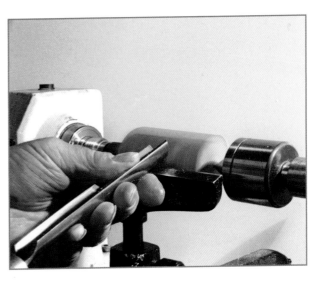

Step 2 Mount the blank between centers on the lathe, taking care to center the points of the drive and revolving center at the center point where the different woods meet. Turn to a cylinder using a spindle roughing gouge.

Step 3 Mount the cylindrical blank in a chuck or in the vise of your pillar drill and carefully drill a 27/64-in. hole down the center. The final appearance of your work will depend upon the accuracy of the drilling, so take great care at this stage.

Step 4 Mark up the blank divided into four sections each approximately one quarter of the length of the pen tube. Number or letter the sections so they do not get out of order. Remember to leave a little leeway on each end for trimming square later and to allow for the thickness of your saw blade. Using a bandsaw, tablesaw, or miter saw, cut the blank into four sections.

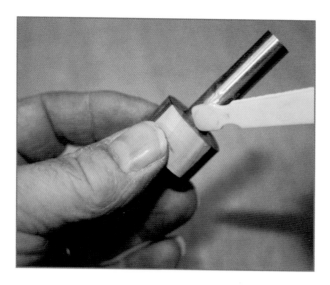

Step 5 Mix up a batch of epoxy adhesive and thoroughly coat one end of the brass tube with the glue. Slide on the first segment of blank and then "butter" the end of it with epoxy. Slide on the next segment, aligning it so that the different woods form a checkerboard pattern. Continue in this manner until all four segments are securely glued in place. You can use CA glue for this process but I prefer epoxy.

Step 6 With all the segments in place, carefully remove any excess glue; check the alignment is accurate and clamp up until the epoxy sets. I prefer to leave the clamped up work overnight, even with quick-setting epoxy, to make sure it is completely cured before beginning any further work on the piece. Once the adhesive is fully cured, trim the ends of the blank square with a barrel trimmer. The ends of the brass tube should be exactly flush with the wood.

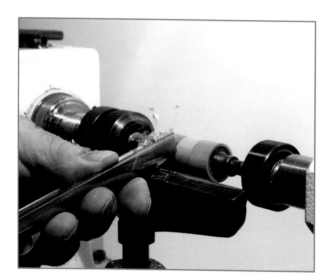

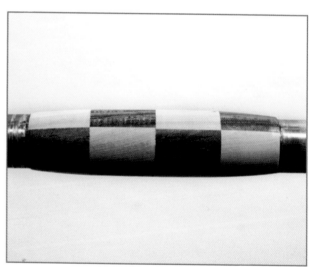

Step 7 Mount the prepared blank on the lathe using the mandrel and bushings; turn down to a cylinder a little larger than the bushings with the roughing gouge and then shape with a skew chisel or Spindlemaster.

Step 8 Once the skew chisel work is completed, the blank should appear as in the photo, and only light sanding should be required to prepare it for finishing. Work through the grits of aluminum oxide abrasive up to 400-grit.

Step 9 The barrel is finished with medium CA, using the technique outlined in Chapter 2. Two or three coats of CA should be applied, followed by sanding through the grits of micromesh and polishing on the buffing wheel with white diamond compound. Here I am wet sanding using micromesh sheets. When wet sanding, it makes sense to protect the lathe bed from moisture with an old towel or rags.

Step 10 Assemble the pencil by screwing the components of the pencil mechanism together with the lower barrel unit and pressing the top and clip unit into the top end of the barrel. The completed barrel is a push fit onto the mechanism, which is then operated by twisting the barrel. The completed pencil can be given a protective coat of microcrystalline wax to protect the finish and prevent fingerprints.

Technical **tip**

With segmented work, the quality of the preparatory work is just as important as the actual turning. Cutting the components square and joining them accurately is vital. When gluing up the blanks and the prepared segments, a few minutes spent sanding the joints to ensure a perfect fit will pay dividends in the final appearance. Fine glue lines will give a fine looking pen, whereas gaps and roughness will spoil your work.

Variations

From top to bottom:

Black & Gold Titanium Sierra Pen in segmented boxwood and rosewood (A)

Rhodium Elegant Beauty Pen in segmented swamp totara and sycamore

Black & Gold Titanium Sierra Pen in segmented boxwood and rosewood (B)

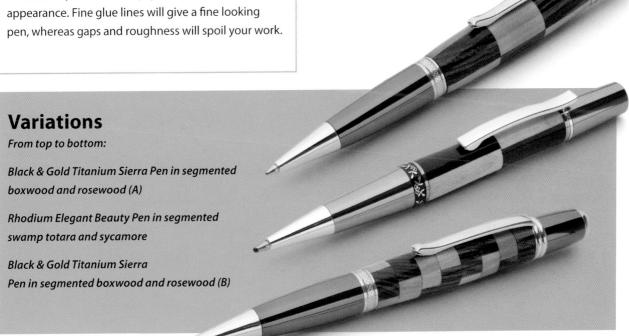

LASER-CUT KILLER WHALE PEN

Laser-cut blanks are rather like three-dimensional jigsaw puzzles and enable turners to create pens with pictures or patterns that would be difficult, if not impossible, by any other means. They vary in complexity—this killer whale blank is somewhere in the midrange of difficulty—but all come with comprehensive instructions for assembling the parts.

Tools and materials

Sierra Pen kit
Type-A mandrel and bushings for kit
Killer whale laser-cut blank
Skew chisel (or Spindlemaster)
Thin and medium CA and epoxy adhesive
240-, 320-, and 400-grit aluminum oxide abrasive
Micromesh abrasives

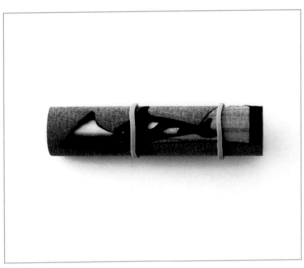

Step 1 Following the manufacturer's instructions, lay out the components and check that your laser-cut kit is complete. I find it helps to lay the parts out on a sheet of white paper or cloth where it is easy to see them and less likely that pieces will get lost on a busy workbench.

Step 2 Begin by assembling the larger components onto the tube as per the instructions. Hold them in place with the supplied rubber bands and slide out the tube. Making sure all the parts are still aligned properly, flood all the joints between the components with CA instant glue. Leave this for a few minutes to set.

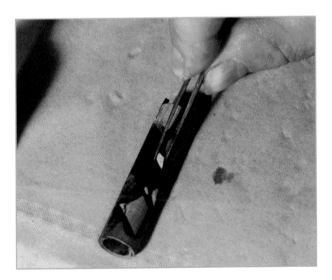

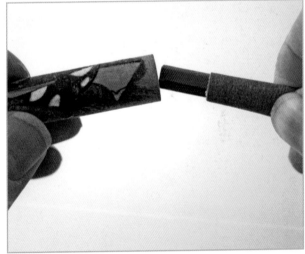

Step 3 Once the main body of the blank is assembled you can begin to insert the smaller components. Some of these are quite tiny, so I use a pair of tweezers to make handling them easier. Working in an uncluttered area on a plain surface will help to make sure any dropped pieces can be found. A lost piece can mean a ruined kit. Each piece must be glued in place by flooding the joints with CA as in Step 2.

Step 4 Once all the components are in place I have a quick check to ensure there are no dry joints and flood any I am unsure about. The blank can now be left to set completely. Once the CA is fully hardened, you may find that the inside of the blank has raised areas that prevent the brass tube from sliding in easily. A little work with some 240-grit abrasive wrapped around a pencil or dowel will ensure a good fit. Do not force the tube; take time to make it fit well.

Step 5 Lightly sand the brass tube in the usual way then glue it in place with epoxy, following the manufacturer's instructions for alignment. Leave the epoxy to harden—the time this takes will vary depending on the brand of epoxy you use but I find it best to leave overnight to ensure it is really firmly set. The ends of the blank now need to be sanded back true to the end of the tube. You cannot use a barrel trimmer for this as the blank will just shatter, so a disk sander or similar is required. Here I am doing this freehand, but it is better to use a jig for accuracy.

Step 6 The completed blank and bushings can now be mounted on a suitable mandrel. In this photo I am using a collet chuck type. You can now begin to turn to size. I do not use a roughing gouge on these kits as they are very delicate and small parts can be dislodged easily.

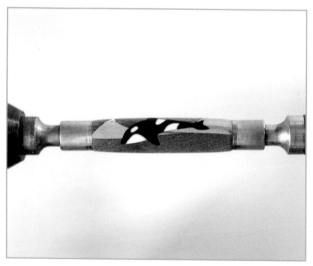

Step 7 Using a skew chisel, begin to shape the blank. Notice the alignment of the tool and how the cutting edge is positioned. The cut should be made about one third of the way up from the bottom edge of the skew, keeping both points well clear of the workpiece. See also how fine the shavings are. Light cuts only are required. If you are not confident using the skew then a Spindlemaster is a suitable alternative.

Step 8 Once you have achieved the desired shape, sand the blank through the grits to 400. If your skew work was fine enough, you should be able to start with 320-grit. Once sanded, the blank can be finished with CA as described in Chapter 2 and then wet sanded with micromesh to a finish.

Technical **tip**

Laser-cut kit designs are all individual and the method of making up the blank varies considerably depending upon the design. The method described here closely follows the manufacturer's instructions for this particular kit, but if you choose a different design you should make sure that you follow the instructions provided. Pay particular attention to the order of assembly and to using the recommended type of adhesive for each stage.

Step 9 The final stage is to buff to a high gloss with white diamond compound on a buffing wheel before assembling the Sierra kit as described in Project No. 2 (see p. 80).

Variations

From top to bottom:

Laser-Cut Fisherman Sierra Click Pen

Laser-Cut Golfers Sierra Twist Pen

Laser-Cut Polar Bears Sierra Twist Pen

Perfect Fit Convertible Pen and Pencil Set

The Perfect Fit Convertible kit is supplied as a ballpoint pen with a twist action. By replacing the refill with the optional pencil twist mechanism it can easily be converted to a mechanical pencil. This project uses a pair of kits to create an attractive pen and pencil set in English yew wood.

Tools and materials

Two Perfect Fit Convertible kits
Type-B mandrel and bushings for kit
11/32-in. and O drill bits
**English yew blanks 6 in. (150mm) long
    by ¾ in. (20mm) square**
Barrel trimmer
Roughing gouge, skew chisel, and parting tool
CA glue for fitting the tubes and finishing
240- and 320-grit aluminum oxide abrasive
Micromesh abrasives

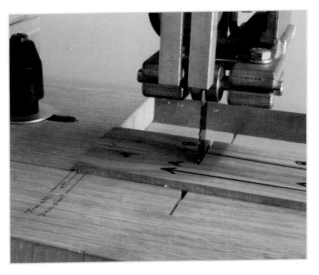

Step 1 Begin by selecting two matching wooden blanks. For this project I have chosen two pieces of English yew that have been cut from the same board and are a mirror image of each other. Yew has a tendency to contain splits and shakes, so choose your stock carefully. Start by marking up the blanks, identifying them as A and B and indicating with an arrow the end that will be the top (cap end). This will ensure that the figure remains aligned and the blanks do not get mixed up during preparation.

Step 2 Cut the blanks to length, leaving them a little longer than the tubes to allow for squaring with a barrel trimmer. Here I am using a shopmade jig on the bandsaw to ensure the blanks are cut square and to accurate length.

Step 3 Now drill the blanks to fit the tubes. The shorter blank, which will form the cap end should be drilled using an 11/32-in. drill bit, while the longer one, for the body, requires a letter O drill bit. Here the blank is mounted in a scroll chuck fitted with engineering jaws. Note that drilling should always begin from the end that will be in the center of the pen as indicated by the marked lines. This will ensure the best alignment of the figure, even if the drill runs off slightly.

Step 4 Lightly scuff the brass tubes with abrasive paper before gluing them in place with your choice of adhesive. For this project I used CA but epoxy or polyurethane glue would be fine too. Once fully set, the blanks can be trimmed square using one of the methods described in Chapter 3. In this photo a blank, held in my shopmade clamp, is being squared off using a barrel trimmer mounted in a keyless chuck on the lathe. A slow speed will produce the best results.

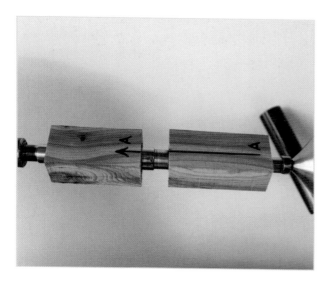

Step 5 One set of the prepared blanks can now be mounted on a type-B mandrel using the appropriate bushings. Take care to get the bushings in the right order by checking against the pen components. Do not fully tighten the mandrel nut until you have mounted the mandrel in the lathe headstock and brought up the revolving tailstock center. Here the blanks and bushings have been mounted and properly aligned on the mandrel.

Step 6 With the lathe running at about 1,800 rpm, you can now begin to turn the blanks down using a spindle roughing gouge, first to a cylinder shape and then to a smooth curve between the bushings. Do not turn right down to the bushings at this stage but allow a little clearance for final shaping and sanding. Take care to use good tool technique—set the tool firmly on the rest, rub the bevel, and gently lift the handle until the tool begins to cut. Take light cuts and keep your gouge sharp.

Step 7 Photo 7 shows the blank roughly turned to shape with gentle curves from the broadest point in the center of the pen out toward the ends. Try to achieve a nice flowing shape that is neither too bulbous nor angular and remember that you will need to make the matching pair as near to the same shape as possible.

Step 8 Once happy with the shape, you can begin to bring the barrels to their finished shape with a skew chisel. Here, a ¾-in. (20-mm) oval skew is positioned for a clean cut about one third of the way from the bottom of the bevel. Do not let the upper half of the bevel or the point of the skew engage with the work or you will have a bad catch. A Spindlemaster can be used if you prefer. It is also possible to use the skew chisel flat on the tool rest as a negative rake scraper, but light cuts are still essential.

Step 9 Once the shape is finalized, only light sanding should be required to prepare the blank for finishing. Here I am beginning the process with 320-grit, but 240-grit may be required to remove any minor irregularities. Continue sanding through the grits to 400. Sand first with the lathe running at a moderate speed (about 1,000 rpm) to avoid overheating the work. Then stop the lathe and sand with the grain to remove any circular scratch pattern before wiping or brushing away the sanding dust and moving on to the next grit.

Step 10 Once sanding is completed, the upper barrel (cap end) needs to be trimmed back to accept the center band. Measure 1⅞ in. (47mm) from the clip end of the barrel and, using the point of a sharp skew chisel, mark the position of the cut. Using a skew chisel will sever the fibers and ensure a clean cut. Then use a parting tool to cut away a rebate all the way through to the brass tube.

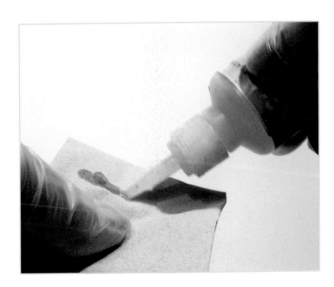

Step 11 The barrels are now ready for you to start applying a finish. For this project I have used a CA (instant glue) finish. With the lathe running at about 500 rpm, begin by applying a drop of boiled linseed oil on a paper towel to bring out the figure. Then, wearing disposable vinyl or latex gloves, apply a line of medium CA to the paper towel as shown here.

Step 12 With the lathe running at 500 rpm, apply CA to one of the barrels in a side-to-side motion until you have even coverage. Repeat for the other barrel. Once dry, apply another two coats of CA in the same way. Allow this to harden for a few minutes and then polish with micromesh, working through the grits to 12,000. Only a light touch is needed with each grit or you may remove the finish. Apply plastic polish using a soft cloth or on a buffing wheel and the first set of barrels is complete.

Step 13 Now repeat Steps 5 to 12 for the second kit. Take care to match the shape of the barrels to the first one. Once both sets of barrels are complete, lay out all of the components ready for assembly. I have made a simple board to facilitate this by cutting a series of V-shaped grooves in a piece of MDF with a router. When laid out neatly like this, is it easy to see how the parts should go together.

Step 14 Begin by pressing the nib into the narrowest end of the lower barrel using one of the methods described in Chapter 2. Here I am using a bench vise, but if you use this method regularly you should protect the vise jaws from the metal components with wooden or MDF jaw plates. Next, press the twist holder into the other end of the blank. I have used a metal tube to protect the end of the twist holder; do not press on the end directly as it is not strong enough and will deform. A wooden spacer with a ⅜-in. hole drilled in it would work just as well.

Step 15 The refill or pencil mechanism can now be inserted and the twist mechanism screwed into place. The pencil mechanism does not require the spring that is supplied with the refill. Test that the pen or pencil is working properly and set the completed part aside.

Step 16 Now assemble the three parts of the center band and press the center band onto the brass tube. I sometimes find a tiny drop of CA glue is required on the brass tube to ensure a firm fit. Press the brass insert into the clip end of the barrel until it is flush and then screw on the cap and clip.

Step 17 The two parts of the pen and pencil can now be pressed together by hand and given a final check. Your set is now complete and ready for use.

Step 18 An attractive set of writing instruments deserves to be displayed properly whether it is for your own use or to be sold or given as a gift. Here the set is shown in an attractive but reasonably inexpensive mahogany colored wooden pen case. Many options are available, from plastic boxes to expensive leather cases, so you can match the quality of presentation to the quality of the product.

Technical **tip**

When making pens and pencils with two-part barrels like these, it is important for appearance that the figure of the wood or the pattern in the acrylic follows through between the two halves. To ensure that this happens, press the parts of one barrel together first. Then screw in the joining component from the other barrel, press the other barrel on lightly by hand so the grain matches, and then unscrew and press fully home.

Variation

Perfect Fit Pen and Pencil Set in Midnight Reef acrylic

Clear Cast Sierra Twist Pen

Clear casting allows you to design your own pen barrels using any thin material—the only limit to what you can use is your imagination. Anything from postage stamps to snakeskin, carbon fiber to computer circuit boards is possible. The casting materials are available as a kit, which is great for the beginner.

Tools and materials

Clear casting resin

Hardener

Measuring cup

4-oz. (115-g) plastic mold

Stirring sticks

Corks or stoppers to seal tube ends

Ball bearings (weights)

Pen kit or kits

Mandrel and bushings for kit

Barrel trimmer

Roughing gouge and skew chisel (or Spindlemaster)

240-, 320-, and 400-grit aluminum oxide abrasive

Micromesh abrasives

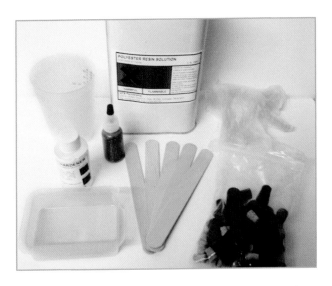

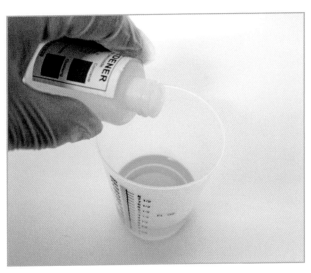

Step 1 Begin by assembling all the materials you will need for casting and prepare an area that is clean and free from dust. Protect surfaces with newspaper or paper towels and have plenty of paper towels or rags to hand to deal with spills and cleaning of equipment. You will need to work quickly but carefully and methodically, as the resin mixture begins to set in about 10 minutes.

Step 2 I strongly recommend you wear disposable gloves for this part of the process. Pour 1 oz. (28g) of the clear casting resin into the measuring cup and add a few drops of hardener in accordance with the manufacturer's instructions. The exact quantity will vary between brands and according to the temperature of your working environment.

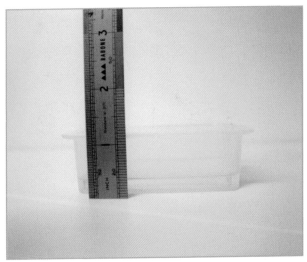

Step 3 Gently stir the mixture with a stirring stick, taking great care not to introduce air into the mix as this will cause bubbles. Once the resin is thoroughly mixed, any bubbles must be carefully removed with the stirring stick.

Step 4 Once the mix is free from bubbles, pour it into the mold until there is a layer about ¼ in. (6mm) thick. Discard any surplus mix and clean out the measuring cup immediately so that it can be re-used. Check the mold again for air bubbles and remove any that appear. You may need to do this a few times, but stop when the mixture begins to cure. Leave this layer to cure for a few hours or overnight. Make sure the mold is left in a location where it will not be contaminated by dust or other particles.

Step 5 While the first stage of the casting cures you can prepare the pen tubes for the next stage. For this project I printed out parts of a large scale map onto self-adhesive labels, but you can be as creative as you like. If you can glue it to a tube, you can clear cast it. Do make sure whatever you use is firmly fixed to the tube—trust me, you do not want bits coming off into the mix or it will ruin your project. Trying to remove or re-fix loose components in a mold of resin mix can get very messy indeed.

Step 6 To prevent the tubes from filling with resin mix they need to be sealed with corks or bungs. Begin by pressing a bung firmly into one end of each tube.

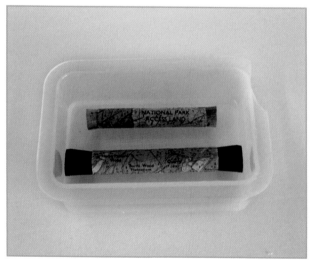

Step 7 The tubes also need to be weighted down to prevent them from floating in the resin mix. This is best done with small ball-bearings as supplied with the clear casting kits. Pour the bearings into each tube, taking care to leave room for the second bung. Seal off the second end of each of the tubes and set them aside until the resin in the mold is cured.

Step 8 Once the resin mix is set, place the prepared tubes carefully on the surface, parallel to the sides and spaced so that each is in the center of one half of the mold as shown.

Step 9 Repeat Steps 2 and 3 but this time using 2 oz. (56g) of resin. Don't forget to make sure this mix is free from bubbles. Pour resin mix over the tubes in the mold until they are nearly, but not completely, covered. Gently roll the tubes from side to side to release any air trapped and make sure they are still properly positioned. Once again, discard any surplus mix and clean out the measuring cup. Keep checking for air bubbles until the mix begins to cure. The resin now needs to be left to cure for 24 hours.

Step 10 Now, using 2 oz. (56g) of resin, again repeat Steps 2 and 3. Fill the mold carefully with the mix, discard any surplus resin, and clean out the measuring cup. As before, keep checking for air bubbles until the mix begins to cure. Set aside to cure.

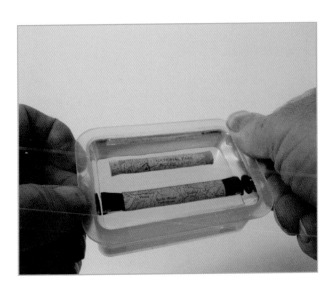

Step 11 After 24 hours the resin mix will be fully cured. Do not be tempted to move on to the next stage until it is fully set. The cast block can now be released by gently twisting the mold from side to side. If you take care, the block should come away cleanly so that the mold can be reused.

Step 12 The block can now be separated into two blanks by cutting on a bandsaw. Note that I am using the fence to guide the block and using a push stick for safety. Take care to cut exactly halfway between the two tubes.

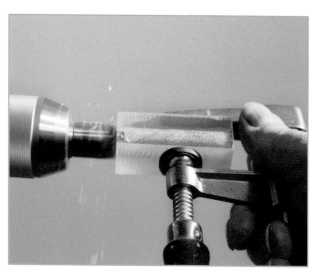

Step 13 Cut one end off each blank, enough to expose the cork or bung that was used to seal the tube; about ⅛ in. (3mm) from the end of the brass tube is about right. Pry out the remaining sealing material and recover the ball-bearing weights for future use. Cut off the other end of the blank and remove the remaining bung.

Step 14 Using a slow speed to avoid chipping the resin blank, trim the end square and back to the brass tube. Here I am using a barrel trimmer mounted on the lathe and I am holding the blank with a small cramp for safety. Other possible methods of doing this are shown in Chapter 2.

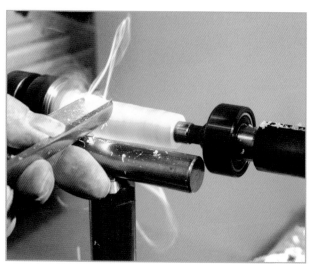

Step 15 You are now ready to turn the completed blanks. Begin by mounting them on a suitable mandrel with bushings appropriate to the pen or pencil kit you have chosen. Here I am using an adjustable mandrel and mandrel saver. Follow my guidance for mounting given in the Work-Holding section of Chapter 2 (see p. 56) and check carefully that everything is running true.

Step 16 Polyester resin is a more brittle material to turn than wood or most acrylics, so make sure that your tools are sharp and take light cuts. You may need to rehone your tools regularly as you work to ensure a clean cut and avoid chipping. Begin by turning to a cylinder with a roughing gouge.

Step 17 Once the barrels are turned almost to size, carefully refine the surface with a skew chisel in preparation for sanding and finishing, using the skew to take very light cuts. Alternatively, the skew may be used in scraping mode as described in Chapter 2.

Step 18 Once the blank is turned to shape, sand through the grits of aluminum oxide abrasive from 240 to 400 to remove any imperfections, and then bring to a finish with micromesh to 12,000-grit. Polyester resin responds well to wet sanding with micromesh but if you use this technique remember to protect your lathe from water with cloths or towels. Finally, buff the blank to a high polish with diamond white compound and a buffing wheel and then press the components together.

Technical **tip**

The methods used for clear casting can also be used to create your own colorful acrylic blanks. By mixing pigments and metallic powders or commercially available materials such as InLace with the resin and hardener mix and casting them in molds in the same way as for clear casting, you can create your own unique designs.

Variations

From top to bottom:

Clear Cast Map Rhodium Elegant Beauty Pen

Rhodium Elegant Beauty Pen with feather blank (cast by Mervyn Cadman)

Rhodium Junior Gentleman's Rollerball with clear cast carbon fiber blank

STREAMLINE DESK PEN

Desk pens are easy to make and the design can be as simple or as elaborate as you choose. Many different pen kits can be modified to fit a pen trumpet, although some, such as the standard Slimline kits, are too slim to fit properly unless modified. This project uses a Streamline kit, similar to the Slimline but with a broader central band.

Tools and materials

Oak pen blank at least 9 in. (230mm) long
Round oak blank 4 in. (100mm) in diameter
  and 2 in. (50mm) thick
Streamline Pen kit
Mandrel and bushings for kit
7-mm drill bit
⅝-in. Forstner bit
Medium CA adhesive
Sanding sealer

Barrel trimmer
Roughing gouge and skew chisel (or Spindlemaster)
⅜-in. (9-mm) spindle gouge
½-in. (13-mm) bowl gouge
⅛-in. (3-mm) or ¼-in. (6-mm) parting tool
Multi-tool and round-ended burr (for texturing)
240- and 320-grit aluminum oxide abrasive
Micromesh abrasives

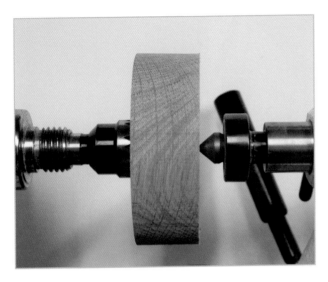

Step 1 Begin by making the desk stand for the pen. The oak blank may be mounted on the lathe in many different ways, for example using a faceplate or screw chuck or by gluing to a wooden faceplate using hot melt glue. I prefer to mount the blank between centers using a drive center in the headstock and a revolving center in the tailstock. I find this method requires less work to remove screw holes or other evidence of the mounting method.

Step 2 Use the ½-in. (13-mm) bowl gouge to turn the blank to round and square up as much of the top face as you can without fouling the revolving center. To true up the face, the long edge of the gouge should be used as shown in Step 7.

Step 3 Again using the bowl gouge, create a smooth curve between the top face and the edge. Work outward from the face to the edge with the flute of the gouge facing the direction of the cut.

Step 4 Using a parting tool, work a shallow recess for the texturing. For best appearance this should be central across the depth of the stand, rather than central between the end of the curve and the base.

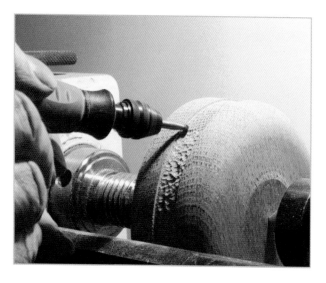

Step 5 With a small round burr fitted to the multi-tool, make random indents to texture the band you have created with the parting tool. Take care not to damage the edges of the groove with the burr. Moving the tool in small circles helps to create a random pattern. Practice first on scrap material until you gain confidence with the technique. Once completed, gently remove any roughness with fine aluminum oxide abrasive and sand the flat part of the edge and the curve through the grits to a finish; 240 to 320-grit will give a suitable finish on oak.

Step 6 The desk stand must now be mounted on the lathe in such a way that the face can be cleaned up and the recess for the pen trumpet created. Here I have used Cole jaws in a scroll chuck, but alternatives such as hot melt gluing to a faceplate or using a Longworth chuck, vacuum chuck, or shopmade jam chuck would work just as well.

Step 7 The top face of the stand should now be trued up using the bowl gouge. Position the tool rest so that the lower long edge of the gouge is level with the center of the work. With the flute of the gouge facing the work and angled in the direction of the cut, bring the lower edge into contact with the center and, taking only light cuts, draw it toward the edge. Don't allow the top edge of the gouge to come into contact. Here the correct positioning of the gouge is shown.

Step 8 The recess for the base of the pen trumpet can be cut using a parting tool, but as the trumpet I was using was exactly ⅝ in. (16mm) in diameter, it was easy to ensure an accurate fit by using a Forstner bit. Take care to make the recess exactly the same depth as the base of the trumpet.

Step 9 The stand must now be reversed in whatever holding device you are using so that the base can be flattened and all evidence of screw holes or marks from the drive center removed. I like to make the base slightly concave so that it stands firmly and does not rock. Use the same technique as for the top face in Step 7.

Step 10 The stand can now be finished in whatever way you choose. This one was polished on a buffing wheel using white diamond compound followed by carnauba wax. The trumpet is then glued into the recess using CA or epoxy adhesive.

Step 11 Now the desk stand is completed we can start work on the pen. The first task is to prepare the blank by cutting the barrel for the nib end to length. Use the brass tube to gauge the length required, leaving sufficient excess for trimming. (The slightly longer tube in the Streamline kit is for the nib end.)

Step 12 The shorter blank can now be drilled through in the normal way, and what will become the lower end of the longer blank should be drilled out just a little deeper than the length of the brass tube. Careful setting up and drilling will be required to ensure accuracy with such a long blank. The dedicated pen blank drilling chuck used here is perfect for the job. Glue the tubes in place with CA or epoxy and when the glue has set trim them square using a barrel trimmer.

Step 13 Mount the blank for the nib end onto the mandrel using the bushings and turn it to shape using a roughing gouge and/or skew chisel. Check the shape regularly by inserting the blank into the pen trumpet and continue shaping until a good fit is achieved. Take care that in fitting to the trumpet you do not turn down the ends too far and spoil the fit with the other components.

Step 14 Once you are happy with the shape, sand smooth and finish with CA or whatever other finish you prefer. Polish with micromesh and buff to a fine finish.

Step 15 Once complete, the nib unit and mechanism can be fitted, the refill inserted and tested for fit, and the center band slipped over the mechanism. The completed lower barrel and stand can now be set aside while the upper barrel is being completed.

Step 16 The blank that will form the upper body of the pen cannot be mounted on a mandrel in the normal way; it is mounted, with the center bushing, onto an adjustable mandrel that is set to the length of the brass tube and then held in place directly by means of a revolving center in the tailstock.

Step 17 Turn the blank to a cylinder using the spindle roughing gouge. If your lathe has a short tool rest, take care not to work off the end of it, but move it along the bed as necessary to reach the full length of the workpiece. Continue turning until the blank is almost down to the diameter of the bushing.

Step 18 Use a parting tool to cut grooves that will delineate each end of the textured band. Do not make these grooves too deep, especially at the lower end where the brass tube is fitted—you do not want the texturing to expose the tube.

Step 19 With a skew chisel, carefully turn down the section between the grooves to the same depth as the grooves. You may need to support the work from behind with your fingers as shown here in order to avoid flexing or vibration.

Step 20 With the round-ended burr once again fitted in the multi-tool (here I am using the multi-tool with a flexible drive shaft, which is easier to manipulate for fine work) and with the lathe stationary, texture the surface in the same way as you did with the stand. As before, take care not to damage the edges of the recess as you work.

Step 21 With the spindle gouge, turn the coves and other decoration on the barrel but do not complete the ball end at this stage.

Step 22 Sand the work on the barrel so far to a fine finish, working through the grits of aluminum oxide abrasive. Check the fit to the bushing, adjusting if necessary with the skew chisel, and then apply a coat of sanding sealer.

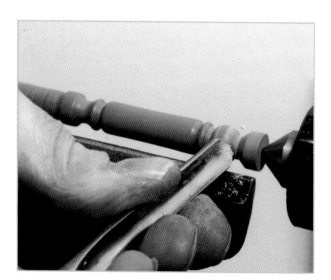

Step 23 Using the spindle gouge once again, turn the ball end of the pen to shape. Take care not to accidentally cut all the way through and part it off prematurely.

Step 24 Sand the partially completed ball to a finish before carefully parting off using the point of the skew chisel and supporting the work with your fingers. Once parted off, the sanding of the ball can be completed by hand and a coat of sanding sealer applied.

Step 25 Once this pen was completed I decided that the design was a little top heavy so I returned it to the lathe to re-work the top section. If you find you need to remount the work for any reason you can do so using a revolving cup center as I have done here.

Step 26 The final stage is to bring the completed barrel to a finish by polishing on a buffing wheel using white diamond compound followed by carnauba wax. This finish is particularly suitable for the textured work and is quite durable enough for this part of the pen, which will not be handled as frequently as the nib section. The completed barrel is simply a push fit onto the lower part of the pen.

Technical **tip**
When making pens that have a closed end and cannot be held on the mandrel in the normal way, it is possible to purchase special mandrels that expand inside the tubes and hold the work. I find it just as effective to hold the work between centers, parting off the closed end at the last minute, and make wooden "jam chuck"-type spigots to hold the barrels while finishing.

Variations
From top to bottom:

Desk pen in reclaimed Brazilian mahogany from Gold Streamline Pen kit

Textured and ebonized desk pen in reclaimed mahogany and rimu from Gold Streamline Pen kit

Pen in applewood from Gold Streamline Pen kit

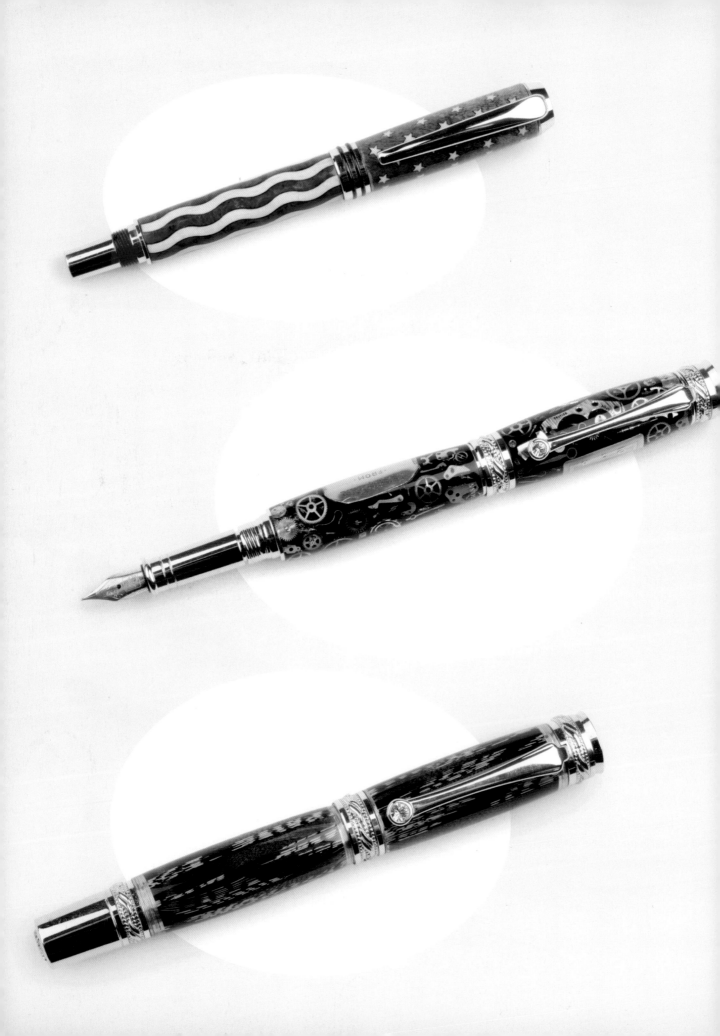

CHAPTER FOUR
GALLERY

KURT HERTZOG

Kurt Hertzog is a professional wood turner, one of the five council members of the Pen Makers Guild, and a member of the board of Directors of the American Association of Woodturners. As well as demonstrating and instructing, Kurt has a keen interest in advanced pen making.

Desk pen made from rattlesnake skin under polyester resin. Nib and top end turned from black Corian®.

Demonstration desk pen made at the Segmented Symposium at Arrowmont Schools of Arts in the U.S. The lengthened blank is constructed from walnut, yellowheart, and maple.

Desk pen made from walnut, maple, black veneer, and cherry. Nib turned from Corian.

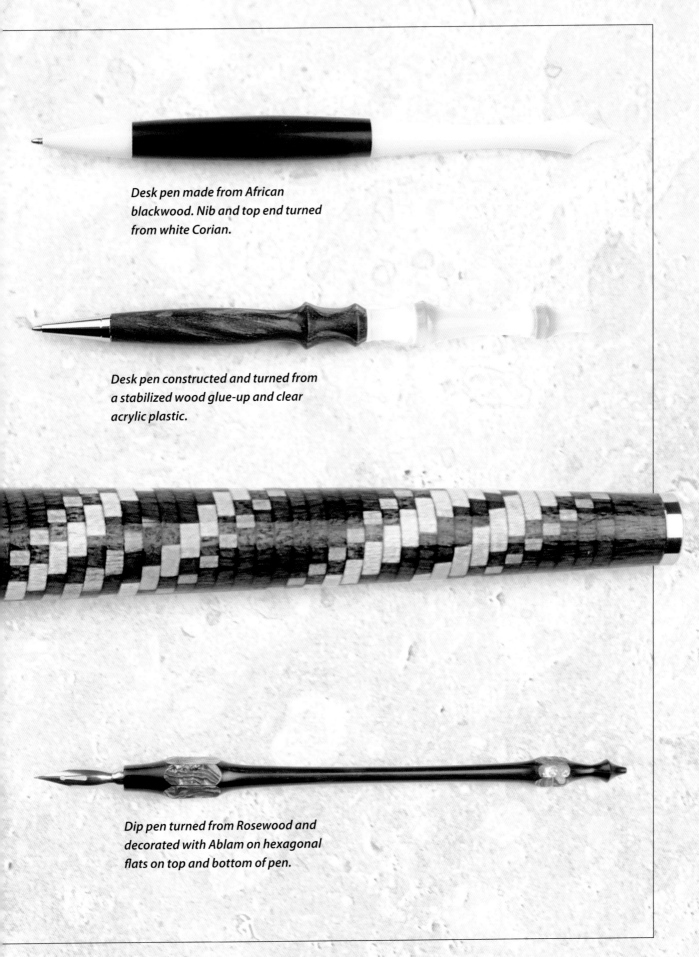

Desk pen made from African blackwood. Nib and top end turned from white Corian.

Desk pen constructed and turned from a stabilized wood glue-up and clear acrylic plastic.

Dip pen turned from Rosewood and decorated with Ablam on hexagonal flats on top and bottom of pen.

Desk pen turned in African blackwood. The fountain pen components and Schmidt reservoir used are from a kit. Forms part of the Jekyll and Hyde desk set.

Desk pen turned from cherry and then painted.

Desk pen turned from cherry and then painted.

Desk pen turned from cherry, carved, and painted. Forms other part of the Jekyll and Hyde desk set.

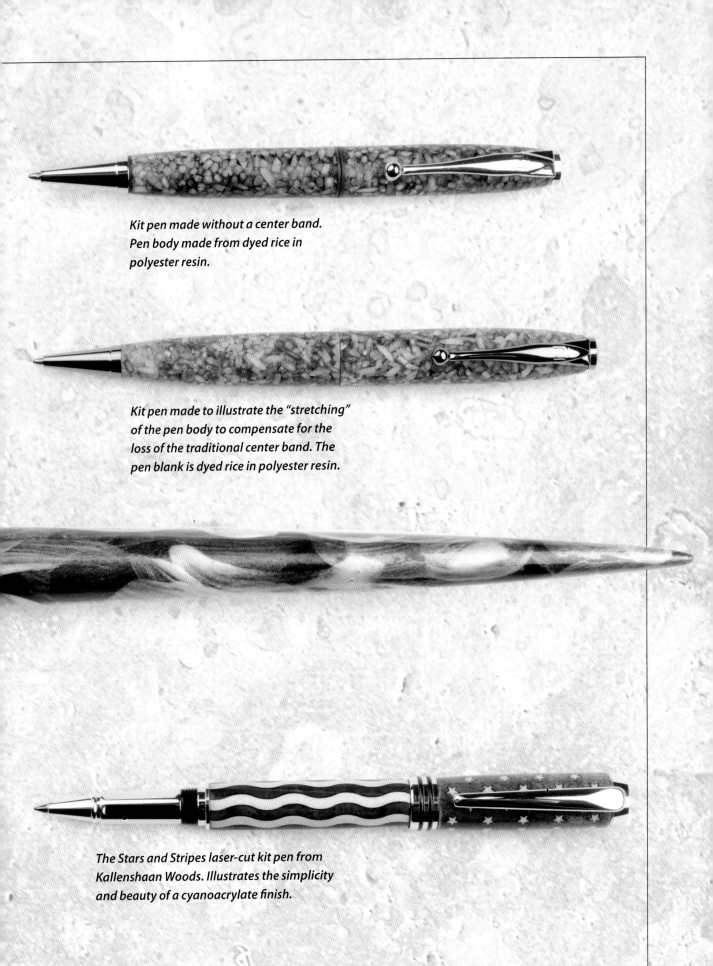

Kit pen made without a center band.
Pen body made from dyed rice in
polyester resin.

Kit pen made to illustrate the "stretching"
of the pen body to compensate for the
loss of the traditional center band. The
pen blank is dyed rice in polyester resin.

The Stars and Stripes laser-cut kit pen from
Kallenshaan Woods. Illustrates the simplicity
and beauty of a cyanoacrylate finish.

BARRY GROSS

Barry Gross is a member of the Pen Makers Guild and has over 30 years of experience as a craftsman. He has published several books and DVDs, and his fine writing instruments are owned by many famous people. He has recently received a Readers' Choice Award from *Pen World* magazine for his work with recycled material.

Ink gel pen made with fly-fishing lure.

Fountain pen made with beer caps.

Ink gel pen made with abalone shells.

Le Chameau shipwreck pen with French coin dated 1725.

Faversham shipwreck pen with Spanish coin dated 1671.

Hamilton watch-pieces pen.

White Breitling dial watch-pieces ink gel pen.

Rex Burningham

Rex Burningham is a nationally recognized wood turner who teaches and demonstrates throughout the U.S. As Vice President of Product Development for Craft Supplies USA, Rex has done much research and development work with pen kits and is widely considered an expert in the field.

Fountain pen made in pink ivory.

Fountain pen made in box elder burl.

Fountain pen made in blackwood.

Twist pen made in stabilized, spalted madrone burl with blackwood center band.

Twist pen made in stabilized, spalted buckeye burl with blackwood center band.

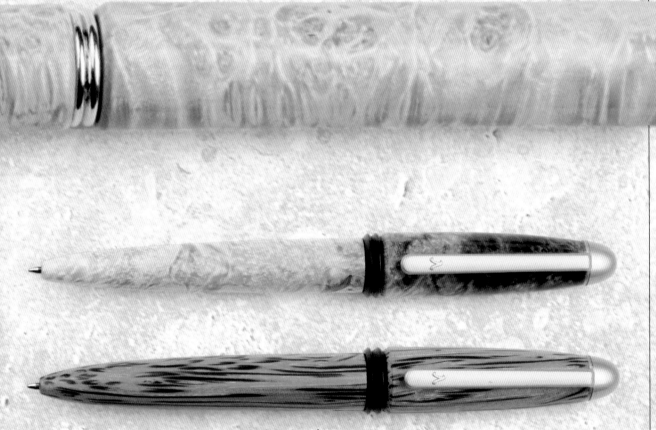

Twist pens made in stabilized box elder burl (above) and stabilized red palm (below). Both with blackwood center bands.

KIP CHRISTENSEN

Kip Christensen is a Professor of Technology and Engineering Education and co-ordinator of the woodworking technology program at Brigham Young University in Utah, USA. Well known for his lidded containers, Kip is also an expert pen maker and co-author with Rex Burningham of the popular book *Turning Pens and Pencils* and eight DVDs on turning pens and other projects.

All pens shown are made with Sierra pen kits and Fiji wood blanks. These blanks are meticulously selected from burled wood caps and cast in colored resin. These blanks were made by Amazon Exotic Hardwoods in Florida, USA.

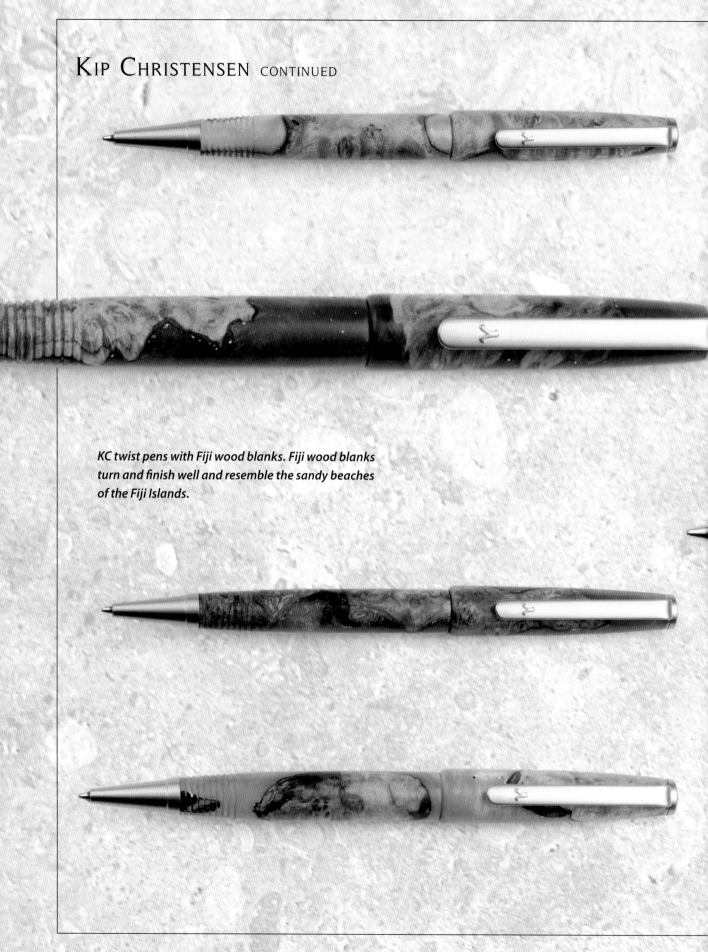

KC twist pens with Fiji wood blanks. Fiji wood blanks turn and finish well and resemble the sandy beaches of the Fiji Islands.

TONI RANSFIELD

Toni Ransfield describes herself as a polymer-clay artist who is addicted to making millefiori canes, beads, finished jewelry, pens, and custom work. Based in the USA, she is widely recognized by pen makers as a leader in the field of polymer clay work.

Polymer clay millefiori pens featuring flowers, bees, ladybugs, and butterflies.

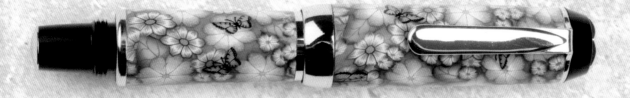

MERVYN CADMAN

Mervyn Cadman is a master in the craft of casting resin/acrylics for pen turning and has come up with some very unusual color effects. He specializes in tying real feathers and then casting them in clear resin. He was recently commissioned by the BBC, in the UK, to cast blanks for five props for the TV series 'Dr Who'.

Elegant Beauty rhodium and titanium gold-plated pen. Cast with grizzly hackle rooster feathers, black acrylic paint, and gold tinsel.

Junior Majestic rhodium roller-ball pen. Cast with Amherst pheasant feathers, red, and black tinsel.

Majestic rhodium, gold-plated, roller-ball pen. Cast with grizzly hackle rooster feathers, blue metallic paint, and blue tinsel.

Majestic rhodium, gold-plated, roller-ball pen. Cast with Amherst pheasant and duck feathers, and gold tinsel.

Gentlemen's clear-cast pen with hand-painted British-style camouflage blank.

Broadwell Art Deco Gold pen in Honduras rosewood with a CA finish.

Retro rhodium-plated pen with cast resin blank in a blue and white swirl.

*Retro black titanium-plated pen with
"Guinness Effect" cast-resin blank.*

*David Broadwell Nouveau Sceptre rhodium
and gold roller-ball pen with Honduras
rosewood blanks with a CA finish.*

*Cigar pen with hand-painted British-style
camouflage blank cast in clear resin.*

*Elegant Beauty rhodium and titanium gold
twist pen with banksia nut blank.*

PHIL IRONS

Phil Irons is highly respected within the wood turning community and is the sole importer for Vicmarc and Woodcut Tools in the UK. He also has his own school of wood turning and enjoys teaching and demonstrating his techniques. Phil's pens are made from the dns-Twister range of kits, for which he is the UK supplier.

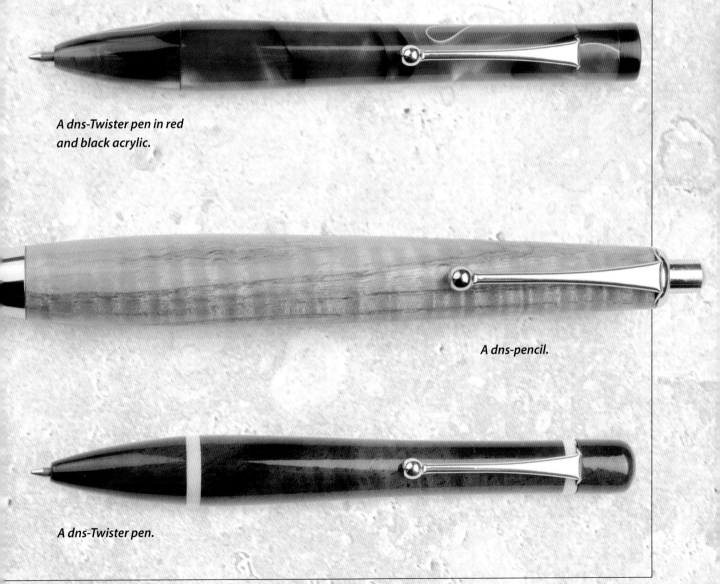

A dns-Twister pen in red and black acrylic.

A dns-pencil.

A dns-Twister pen.

Glossary

Acrylic
The generic term for plastic materials such as polyester resin used to make pen blanks.

Adjustable mandrel
A pen mandrel the length of which can be adjusted to suit the dimensions of the pen being worked upon.

Aluminum oxide
An abrasive material normally with a cloth or paper backing.

Bandsaw
A powered saw used in woodworking and metalworking consisting of a toothed metal band driven around two wheels.

Bevel
Strictly speaking the bevel is the angle between the cutting surface of the tool and the back surface but the term is more generally used to describe that part of the tool that is ground or honed to form the cutting edge.

Blank trimmer
A device consisting of a shaft and cutting head that can be mounted in a lathe or powertool to trim the ends of pen blanks square to the brass tubes.

BLO (boiled linseed oil)
Linseed oil (extracted from flax) that has been heated and to which chemicals have been added to promote quicker drying.

Brad point bit
A drill bit with a sharp spur and two cutting lips useful for cutting across the grain of the timber.

Brass tubes
The tubes that form the sub structure on which pens and pencils are made.

Buffing wheel
See Mop wheel

Bullet point bit
A drill bit with a bullet-shaped spur and ground away flutes that cuts accurately in most materials.

Burl
A rounded deformity in a tree that gives rise to wild and attractive figure within the wood.

Bushings
Metal fittings that are used to mount pen blanks on a mandrel and to indicate the size to which the blank must be turned.

Carbon steel
Steel in which the main alloy component is carbon. Prior to the introduction of high speed steel many turning tools were made from carbon steel.

Carnauba wax
A hard wax from a Brazilian palm tree that is used as a finish.

Catalyst
A chemical used to react with polyester resins and epoxies causing the materials to harden.

Cellulose lacquer
A coating made by dissolving natural resins in a solvent.

Chuck
A device fixed to the lathe spindle or tailstock quill for holding a tool or workpiece.

Clear casting
The process of using polyester resin to create clear forms in which items may be embedded. Can be used to create pen blanks.

Collet chuck
A chuck with a conical insert that can be used to hold cylindrical objects in the lathe.

Cross vise
A vise that can be moved in two planes to accurately position a component.

Crosscut
Cut across the grain of the wood. This can give rise to interesting patterns in the figure of a pen blank.

Cyanoacrylate (CA)
A compound with an acrylate base used as an adhesive and in pen making as a finish.

Dead center
A pointed fitting mounted in the spindle or tailstock of a lathe to support the work.

Diamond hone
A flat sharpening plate embedded with industrial diamonds used to bring a tool to a fine edge.

Disc sander
A powered sanding machine that can, amongst many other uses, be used with a jig to square the ends of pen blanks.

Drill driver
A split Morse taper device used to drive a drill bit or other cylindrical tool such as a pen mandrel.

Drill press
A bench- or floor-mounted drilling machine

Drill stand
A stand for mounting a powerdrill or for use with a suitable vice or holding device for accurate vertical drilling.

Engineering jaws
Stepped jaws normally fitted to an engineering chuck but also useful for holding small items on the wood lathe.

Epoxy adhesive
A two-part adhesive consisting of a resin and a hardener used in pen turning to attach pen blanks to the brass tubes.

Figure
The patterns in wood caused by color variation between the tissues of the wood.

Fixed mandrel
A pen mandrel of fixed length.

Forstner bit
A special drill bit used for drilling flat-bottomed and overlapping holes.

Friction polish
Shellac-based polish applied to a workpiece on the lathe and brought to a finish by burnishing with a cloth.

Grain
The orientation of the fibers relative to the long axis of the timber.

Green wood
Wood that has been cut but not yet dried; generally unsuitable for pen making because of its instability.

Grinder
A powered device consisting of a motor and abrasive grinding wheels commonly used with jigs or by hand to sharpen turning tools.

Grit
A measure used to indicate the coarseness of an abrasive. The higher the grit number the finer the abrasive.

Hardener
See Catalyst

Headstock
That part of the lathe on which the drive spindle is mounted.

High-speed steel (hss)
A steel alloy used for making tools. It combines steel with other metals including, for example, tungsten or chromium to improve wear resistance. It is the best material for turning tools.

Hone
To polish the bevel of a tool so as to provide a sharp cutting edge.

Jacobs chuck
A key-operated chuck commonly used in the tailstock to hold drill bits or in the headstock to hold a mandrel or barrel trimmer.

Jig
A fixture or device used to hold a workpiece or tool to facilitate a particular operation.

Lacquer
A coating that dries by evaporation leaving a glossy surface.

Laminated wood
Wood-based composite material formed from layers of veneers that may be colored or stabilized by the addition of resins.

Laser-cut blanks
Pen blanks formed by a laser cutting process to create patterns or pictures.

Machine vise
A vise designed to be mounted on a drill press or drill stand to hold the workpiece securely for vertical drilling.

Mandrel
A device used to mount the pen blanks on the lathe by means of a Morse taper or attachment to a chuck.

Mandrel saver
A device used to replace the revolving center in a lathe tailstock to support the mandrel and blanks.

Mechanism
The component that provides the motion required to advance or retract the nib or lead from a pen or pencil.

Melamine lacquer
Lacquer made from melamine resin.

Microcrystalline wax
A petrochemical-based wax that due to its chemical structure provides a more durable finish than traditional waxes. Used in pen making over other finishes to prevent fingerprints.

Micromesh abrasive
Abrasives made from abrasive crystals that float on the backing material.

Millefiori
A technique originally used in glass making to produce patterned canes. Used in the making of polymer clay pens.

Mop wheel
Arbor-mounted wheel made from stitched or unstitched cotton or woolen cloth used for polishing.

Morse taper
The tapered shaft of a tool or tapered socket of a lathe head- or tailstock used as a means of mounting lathe tools and workpieces.

Nonwoven abrasive
An abrasive made from nylon or other synthetic fibers and coated with abrasive material.

Parting tool
A narrow-bladed tool used for parting off and cutting grooves.

Pen blank
A prepared wooden or man-made blank of a suitable size for pen making.

Pen blank chuck
A lathe chuck specifically designed for drilling pen blanks.

Pen blank vise
A dedicated vise designed for use with a pillar drill or drill stand to ensure accurate vertical drilling.

Pen press
A dedicated device designed to press the metal components of the pen into the brass tubes.

Pen tube inserter
A tapered tool used to hold tubes for insertion into the blank.

Pen wizard
An ornamental pen-turning device.

Pin jaws
Chuck jaws designed to hold a workpiece by expanding into a drilled hole. May also be used to hold a small workpiece such as a pen blank by compression.

Plating
The thin metal coating that provides the decorative and wear resisting properties of pen components.

Polyester resin
A clear resin used in clear casting and the manufacture of pen blanks.

Polymer clay
A moldable artist's material based on PVC (polyvinylchloride) that can be used for making pen blanks.

Polyurethane glue
Polyurethane-based adhesive.

Revolving center
A device, normally with a pointed end, running on bearings to provide support to the tailstock end of a workpiece.

Safety cloth
A nonwoven paper-based material that will tear if tangled in the work and thereby help prevent injury from hands being drawn into contact with the revolving workpiece or machine.

Safety glasses
Spectacles with toughened lenses to protect against debris.

Sanding sealer
Cellulose- or shellac-based compound for sealing wood prior to or during sanding.

Scroll saw
Mechanical saw with a reciprocating blade for decorative work.

Silicone carbide
An abrasive material commonly used in car body finishing.

Skew chisel
Turning tool with a skewed cutting surface useful for spindle work and fine finishing of pen barrels.

Solid surface material
Man-made material of polyester and acrylic resins used for worktops but from which it is possible to create pen blanks.

Spindle
The revolving component of the lathe headstock onto which tools and workpieces are mounted by means of a screw thread or Morse taper.

Spindle gouge
A gouge used for forming beads, coves, and other spindle work.

Spindle roughing gouge
A gouge used primarily in spindle work for bringing rough wood to a cylinder.

Split mandrel
A design of mandrel divided into two components that fit into the head- and tailstock to hold the workpiece.

Stabilized wood
Wood that has been treated with resins to minimize breakout and splintering. Mostly used with burls and other fragile woods.

Tailstock
The lathe component that supports the nondriven end of the workpiece or in which drills or other tools may be mounted.

Tailstock quill
The shaft of the tailstock, usually hollow with a Morse taper socket and threaded for lateral movement.

Tool rest
Part of the lathe that provides support to the turning tool.

Tool rest base
The part of the lathe that is mounted on the lathe bed to support the tool rest and can be adjusted to determine its position.

Transfer punch
A cylindrical punch used in engineering, supplied in a range of sizes that are useful for dismantling pens for repair work.

Tripoli
Medium to fine polishing compound.

Twist drill bit
A spirally fluted drill bit primarily designed for metal working but useful for drilling all forms of pen blank.

Variable speed
An electronic or mechanical system for continuously varying the speed of the lathe to suit the task in hand.

White diamond
Fine polishing compound.

Suppliers

UK

Axminster Tool Centre

Tools and machinery, pen kits, blanks

Trafalgar Way

Axminster

Devon

EX13 5PB

Tel: (Toll free) 0800 371822

Web: www.axminster.co.uk

Craft Supplies

Tools, pen kits, blanks

Newburgh Works

Netherside

Bradwell

Derbyshire

S33 9JL

Tel: +44 (0) 1433 622550

Web: www.craft-supplies.co.uk

Phil Irons Woodturning

Tools and machinery, pen kits

PO Box 5120

Stratford-upon-Avon

Warwickshire

CV37 1JB

Tel: +44 (0) 1789 204052

Web: www.philirons.co.uk

Snainton Woodworking Supplies

Tools and machinery, pen kits, blanks

Barkers Lane

Snainton

Scarborough

North Yorkshire

YO13 9BG

Tel: +44 (0) 1723 859545

Web: www.snaintonwoodworking.com

Stiles and Bates

Tools and machinery, pen kits, blanks

Upper Farm

Church Hill

Sutton

Dover

Kent

CT15 5DF

Tel: +44 (0) 1304 366360

Web: www.stilesandbates.co.uk

Turners Retreat

Tools and machinery, pen kits, blanks

Snape Lane

Harworth

Nottinghamshire

DN11 8NE

Tel: +44 (0) 1302 744344

Web: www.turners-retreat.co.uk

UK Pen Kits

Pen kits, pen blanks, pen-making accessories

3 The Croft

Earls Colne

Colchester

Essex

CO6 2NH

Tel: +44 (0) 7970 398872

Web: www.ukpenkits.com

USA

Beall Tool Company
Tools and equipment
541 Swan's Road N.E.
Newark
Ohio, 43055
Tel: (Toll free) 1-800-331-4718
Web: www.bealltool.com

Bear Tooth Woods
Pen kits, pen blanks, pen-making accessories
PO Box 26674
Colorado Springs
CO 80936
Tel: +1-719-532-1756
Web: www.beartoothwoods.com

Craft Supplies USA
Pen kits, pen blanks, pen making accessories
1287 E. 1120 S.
Provo
UT 84606
Tel: (Toll free) 1-800-551-8876
Web: www.woodturnerscatalog.com

Kallenshaan Woods
Laser-cut blanks, engraving, boxes
940 Crazyhorse Way
Las Vegas
NV 89110
Tel: +1 702-503-9236
Web: www.kallenshaanwoods.com

Lee Valley Tools Ltd
Tools and equipment
P.O. Box 1780
Ogdensburg
NY 13669-6780
Tel: +1 800-871-8158
Web: www.leevalley.com

Penn State Industries
Pen kits, pen blanks, pen making accessories
9900 Global Rd.
Philadelphia
PA 19115
Tel: (Toll free) 1-800-377-7297
Web: www.pennstateind.com

Rockler Woodworking and Hardware
Pen kits, pen blanks, pen-making accessories
4365 Willow Drive
Medina
MN 55340
Tel: +1 800-279-4441
Web: www.rockler.com

Toni Ransfield
Polymer clay millefiori canes and supplies
Web: www.ExclusiveDesignz.com

Woodcraft Supply
Pen kits, pen blanks, pen making accessories
1177 Rosemar Road
P.O. Box 1686
Parksburg, WV 26102
Tel: +1 800-225-1153
Web: www.woodcraft.com

Australia

Timberbits
PO Box 286A
Fairfield Heights
NSW 2165
Tel: +61 (0)2 9711-8926
Web: www.timberbits.com

Carroll's Woodcraft Supplies
66 Murradoc Road
Drysdale
Victoria 3222
Tel: +61 (0)3 5251-3874
Web: www.cws.au.com

RESOURCES

Books

The Pen Turner's Workbook by Barry Gross
(ISBN 978-1-56523-319-5)

Turning Pens and Pencils by Kip Christensen
and Rex Burningham
(ISBN 978-1-86108-100-1)

Turning Wood with Richard Raffan, updated
and expanded third edition
(ISBN 978-1-56158-956-2)

Taunton's Complete Illustrated Guide to Turning
by Richard Raffan
(ISBN 978-1-56158-672-1)

DVDs

Pen Turning by Barry Gross

Turning Acrylic Materials by Barry Gross

Turning Pens: The Basics and Beyond by Kip Christensen and
Rex Burningham

Turning Pens: More Pens plus Tips & Tricks by Kip Christensen
and Rex Burningham

Simple Methods for Superior Turned Pens by Paul Loseby

Websites

The International Association of Penturners
www.penturners.org

The UK Association of Pen Turners
www.ukpenkits.com

Steven Russell's Woodturning Tips Library
www.woodturningvideosplus.com

The Woodworkers Institute
www.woodworkersinstitute.com

IMPERIAL/METRIC CONVERSIONS

Drill and bushing sizes

There are no exact imperial equivalents to metric drill and bushing sizes, which is why they have not been stated in this book. However, by comparing the decimal inch measurement of a metric drill to the decimal inch measurements in the list of imperial drill sizes, the nearest match can be found and the user can decide whether to use a slightly larger or slightly smaller size depending upon the requirements of the job in hand.

Imperial to metric						Metric to imperial	
Inches (fractions)	Inches (decimal)	Millimeters	Inches (fractions)	Inches (decimal)	Millimeters	Millimeters	Inches
1/64	0.0156	0.3969	33/64	0.5156	13.0969	1	0.0394
1/32	0.0313	0.7938	17/32	0.5313	13.4938	1.5	0.0591
3/64	0.0469	1.1906	35/64	0.5469	13.8906	2	0.0787
1/16	0.0625	1.5875	9/16	0.5625	14.2875	2.5	0.0984
5/64	0.0781	1.9844	37/64	0.5781	14.6844	3	0.1181
3/32	0.0938	2.3813	19/32	0.5938	15.0813	3.5	0.1378
7/64	0.1094	2.7781	39/64	0.6094	15.4781	4	0.1575
1/8	0.1250	3.1750	5/8	0.6250	15.8750	4.5	0.1772
9/64	0.1406	3.5719	41/64	0.6406	16.2719	5	0.1969
5/32	0.1563	3.9688	21/32	0.6563	16.6688	5.5	0.2165
11/64	0.1719	4.3656	43/64	0.6719	17.0656	6	0.2362
3/16	0.1875	4.7625	11/16	0.6875	17.4625	6.5	0.2559
13/64	0.2031	5.1594	45/64	0.7031	17.8594	7	0.2756
7/32	0.2188	5.5563	23/32	0.7188	18.2563	7.5	0.2953
15/64	0.2344	5.9531	47/64	0.7344	18.6531	8	0.3150
1/4	0.2500	6.3500	3/4	0.7500	19.0500	8.5	0.3346
17/64	0.2656	6.7469	49/64	0.7656	19.4469	9	0.3543
7/32	0.2813	7.1438	25/32	0.7813	19.8438	9.5	0.3740
19/64	0.2969	7.5406	51/64	0.7969	20.2406	10	0.3937
5/16	0.3125	7.9375	13/16	0.8125	20.6375	10.5	0.4134
21/64	0.3281	8.3344	53/64	0.8281	21.0344	11	0.4331
11/32	0.3438	8.7313	27/32	0.8438	21.4313	11.5	0.4528
23/64	0.3594	9.1281	55/64	0.8594	21.8281	12	0.4724
3/8	0.3750	9.5250	7/8	0.8750	22.2250	12.5	0.4921
25/64	0.3906	9.9219	57/64	0.8906	22.6219	13	0.5118
13/32	0.4063	10.3188	29/32	0.9063	23.0188	13.5	0.5315
27/64	0.4219	10.7156	59/64	0.9219	23.4156	14	0.5512
7/16	0.4375	11.1125	15/16	0.9375	23.8125	14.5	0.5709
29/64	0.4531	11.5094	61/64	0.9531	24.2094	15	0.5906
15/32	0.4688	11.9063	31/32	0.9688	24.6063	15.5	0.6102
31/64	0.4844	12.3031	63/64	0.9844	25.0031	16	0.6299
1/2	0.5000	12.7000	1	1.0000	25.4000	16.5	0.6496

ABOUT THE AUTHOR

Walter Hall has been turning pens and pencils for more than 20 years and is a regular contributor to *Woodturning* magazine. Based in beautiful Northumberland in the UK, Walter sells his bespoke pens and pencils through craft centers and via his Web site: www.walterspens.co.uk

Walter began the hobby of wood turning while working in the British National Health Service as an accountant. Given an old lathe by a friend, he restored it to working order and began to teach himself the basic skills of wood turning. He soon developed a keen interest in pen making and started to sell his pens and pencils to help fund the purchase of better tools and equipment.

Having written a short "beginner's guide to wood turning," which he posted on the forums of the Woodworkers Institute and the UK Association of Pen Turners, Walter began to consider how else he might enable other pen makers to

benefit from the knowledge and skills he had accumulated. From this came the concept of this technical manual with step-by-step projects.

ACKNOWLEDGMENTS

I would not have been able to write this book without the help and support of my family and friends and in particular the encouragement of my wife Edith.

I am also deeply indebted to many friends and colleagues in the wood-turning community for their assistance and advice both in person and through Internet forums. Their practical advice and the inspiration I have derived from their work have been invaluable.

In particular I would like to thank Mark Baker for his encouragement to turn what was originally planned as a short beginner's guide into a much more extensive work

and for checking some of the technical sections, Mervyn Cadman, Colin Gregg, and countless others for their advice on techniques over many years and Toni Ransfield whose generous sharing of her knowledge of polymer clays was fundamental to those sections of the book and upon whose tutorial the polymer clay pen project is based.

Finally, I am deeply indebted to Barry Gross, Kip Christensen, Kurt Hertzog, Mervyn Cadman, Phil Irons, Rex Burningham, and Toni Ransfield, all of whom have kindly agreed to allow their fine writing instruments to be photographed for the gallery section of the book.

INDEX

Names of projects are printed in **bold**.
Illustrated pens and pencils in the Gallery
section are indicated by page numbers
in **bold**.

To place an order or to request a catalog, contact:

The Taunton Press, Inc.
63 South Main Street, P.O. Box 5506, Newtown, CT 06470-5506
Tel: (800) 888-8286

www.taunton.com